What the Sea Means

Books available from Hope and Nonthings:

Incomplete Philosophy Of Hope And Nonthings
Selected plays by ian pierce (a.k.a. John Pierson).   H&N001 $10.00

Half Li(v)es by Anita Loomis
Stories, poems and monologues.   H&N002 $8.00

Like Hell by Ben Weasel
A punk rock novel.   H&N003 $12.00

An Apology for the Course and Outcome of Certain Events Delivered by Doctor John Faustus on This His Final Evening & The Hunchback Variations
by Mickle Maher
Two one act plays.   H&N005 $10.00

Neo Solo: 131 Neo-Futurist Solo Plays from Too Much Light Makes the Baby Go Blind
A book of 131 solo plays written and performed by the cast of
Too Much Light Makes The Baby Go Blind.   H&N007 $15.00

Punk Is A Four-Letter Word by Ben Weasel
Collected essays from a punk rock journalist. Includes previously unreleased material.   H&N008 $12.00

What the Sea Means: Poems, Stories & Monologues 1987-2002
by Dave Awl   H&N009 $12.95

These books can be ordered by mail:

> Hope And Nonthings
> P.O. Box 148010
> Chicago, IL 60614-8010

Add $1.50 postage per item, $2.50 Overseas
Enclose check or money order made out to: Hope And Nonthings

For more information, visit Hope and Nonthings online:
www.hopeandnonthings.com

What the Sea Means

Poems, Stories & Monologues

1987-2002

by
Dave Awl

Hope and Nonthings

All inquiries concerning rights and permissions should be addressed to:
Hope and Nonthings — PO Box 148010, Chicago, IL 60614-8010
Tel: 773-528-5568 Fax: 773-529-4248
www.hopeandnonthings.com

Published by Hope and Nonthings
First Edition September 2002

Dave Awl's Web site: www.ocelotfactory.com

Cover and book design by Lori Dana / Image Studio
Photo credits — Front cover: Pineapple photo by Jim Alexander Newberry.
Laughing Sal photo by Cary Norsworthy. Back cover: Author photo (at Avebury)
by Kurt Heintz. Inside: "Please Drive Slowly" photo by Kurt Heintz.
All other photos by Dave Awl.

Library of Congress Control Number: 2002111009

Awl, Dave
        What the sea means: poems, stories & monologues 1987-2002
        I. Title

ISBN 0-9707458-7-7

For seven teachers:

Marcia Holmes,
Rita Dunn, Judy Murphy,
George Armstrong, Charles Meyer,
Penny Pucelik, and Kevin Stein

CONTENTS

PREFACE..xi
NOTES ON PERFORMANCE AND STAGING xiii
PERFORMANCE AND PUBLICATION HISTORY....................xiv
ACKNOWLEDGEMENTS xv

I. WHAT THE SEA MEANS: POEMS 1998-2002

Zeppo 3
The City Slept and Metal Phantoms 5
Tommy El 7
The Flymaker Sweeps the Shop 8
The New Planet...10
What the Sea Means 2.0 11
Night Passage Home...16
The City You Almost Lived In..17
Letter to Mark in Dublin..19
The Sentence Suspended 22
Moth Song for a New Summer 24
Alas, Hyacinth..25
Critique of the Geometrical State 26
Safe from the Moon 28
Watching Him Dance 29
Glastonbury..30
Dancing With Otto..33
A Perfectly Empty Room..34
Bestiary 36
February: Sometimes Such Disparate Things 51
The Old Flame Sublimated into Hermetic Metaphor..........52
What I Mean to Say: June, 1984 53
Tara 55
Night Diary for a Summer Afternoon 56
Notes from first trip to San Francisco, 1986, 20 years old: found
    scrawled in a spiral notebook fifteen years later 57
Awake While They Sleep..60
Avebury 63

The Reader's Lament 65
First Entry: Sun., Feb. 03, 2002, 11:02 p.m. CST 66
To the Would-Be Shaman of the Urban Age 69
Callanish in August 70
The Legend 72
Judgment and Death of the Super-Villain 73
The DJ Considered as Mage...75
Reservoir 76
Immense Buddha Under Fire...77
The Writer's Prayer 78
Post Script...79
Dooncarton 80
Immensity 82

II. BIG GLASS JAR: MONOLOGUES AND STORIES 1990-1999

The Idea of You 85
Young Person's Guide to Synchronicity 86
A Poverty of Murk..87
The Day of Your Return 88
Story #423 89
Between the Lines in 4/4 Time 90
Jimmy, Roger & John 91
Told Me What? 92
Freedom (for Chuang-tze) 94
Painting for an Empty Canvas 95
Parts of Me Function Like a Dream 96
City Dream #8..98
Please Drive Slowly 100
An American Childhood 101
Justice Takes a Road Trip Part II 102
Stonewalled, or The Sound of the Crowd 103
The Age of Disease Part I 105
Davy Jones in the Produce Department: A Piscean Parable 106
X-Punch 2K 108
The Language Families 110
Points of Connection 111
I ≠ AM 114
Talking to Myself...115

Big Glass Jar, or Pearls Go with Everything 117
Snow 119
Talking to Myself: The Interview..121

III. NIGHT DIARIES: POEMS 1995-1997

January (The Routine) 125
Letter to Christopher 126
At the Turning 127
Letter (4/24/96) 128
Film Loop #12..129
Cameo (March, 1995) 130
Night Diary #3 131
Axolotl 132
Night Diary #2 134
Night Diary #7 135
Lay of the Antimuse 136

IV. THE DESIRES OF GLASS: POEMS 1987-1995

I Am the Man Vermeer Painted Over 139
Stitching a Dummy..140
Glass Insects 142
Laughing Sal 144
Map of the Body 147
The Sideshow..148
Summer Sketch 149
Staring at Orion's Left Foot 150
Nocturne 152
Encountering Astrology at the School Street Café, 1989 153
prince of the forest..154
Letter (Midnight presses an enormous face) 155
Drowsing..156
Sonnet of the Sea Moth 158
The Orchard 160
A Trick of the Light 164
Summer...166
the moment the body feels pain..167
Lisa Goddamn 168
The Buddha Receiving a Gift of Heart-Shaped Chocolates 171

Ban Sidhe Bridge..172
The State of My Life 174
Van Gogh 175
two poems appassionata..177
The Octopus 178
lughnassadh: iii 180
essays on distraction..181
Letter to Carl Jung in Vienna 182
Sonata 183

NOTES 185

Preface

As far back as my cornfield-bound college days, I remember a certain erstwhile literary compatriot of mine picking up one of my spiral-bound notebooks, leafing through it and exclaiming in disgust, "Your poetry always changes!"

Looking back over fifteen years of post-collegiate poetry (and even dipping back into the milk-crate-rustling era for a few poems), it's apparent that yes, there is a certain stylistic instability represented here, a certain pattern of formal infidelity. For some of it I can plead circumstance: Writing for the poetry reading stage is different from writing for the performance stage, and both are different from writing for the streetlights coming in through your window at three a.m. with no regard for the consequences.

Nonetheless I think that, at the hoary age of 36, I've given up the quest to find a consistent poetic style or voice. Such a thing just doesn't appear to be in the cards for me. Maybe it's the Gemini rising or all the planets in my twelfth house. Or in layperson's terms, a certain chronic inability to make up my mind about anything, pick a path, pick *one* CD, pick an appetizer, pick anything.

I tell you this not just to appall you with the questionable spectacle of a poet musing publicly about his own work, but also to explain the regrettable absence of the poetic manifesto with which I would have liked to open this book. I would have loved to produce a thundering declaration of aesthetics to preface this collection like a burst of kettle drums. Something sly, bold and yet also charming, like Frank O'Hara's *Personism: a Manifesto.*

But for me to attempt to sell you a manifesto at this point would be too much like the radio taking credit for the transmission it receives, or maybe the prism for the light it scatters. All I can really acknowledge doing, to the best of my ability, is diligently picking up the receiver each time the muse deigns to dial my number. If I have a philosophy of poetry, it's this: When the muse calls, answer the phone. No matter where you are: on the street corner waiting for the bus, at a restaurant where the table is too small to accommodate your spiral notebook, at a party or a nightclub or the hair salon. Scavenge a scrap of paper if necessary and let the people look at you funny but whatever you do, don't try to put the muse on hold and think she/he/it will put up with that.

Because in my experience, if the muse knows you'll actually sit down at the keyboard or pick up a pen when she sends you an inspiration, you start to hear from her more often. If, on the other hand, you tend not to answer the muse-line because you're on the subway on your way to work, or on deadline with some "deliverable" or other, or busy watching *The Simpsons* and eating Tater Tots, well, the muse gets a little affronted and decides to send her business where it's better appreciated, and one day you notice she's not calling you so often any more.

My muse-whipped dependence on fits of inspiration may in itself explain the lack of stylistic coherence in these pages: The truth is, I don't choose my poems, they choose me. I try to let each piece take on the form that suits it best, and not worry about dressing it like the other kids in the class. This book is nothing like the one I would have consciously conceived and planned, not anything like the volume I imagined one day producing back in my college years. It's lumpy, given to spasms of gauche whimsy and outbursts of disruptive surrealism, and its socks don't match its shirt. But these are the poems that came to the party, the boys who liked me enough to kiss me, the ones who were willing to be seen with me in public. How can I not stand by them in light of that, no matter how lopsided or eccentric or lacking in the streamlined grace of the imaginary lover?

When they put their arms around me, I forget to gaze over their shoulders at the unattainable, and I relax into the dance, and if it's not the nirvana of conjecture it's also better in subtle and surprising ways, because it has weight, and texture, and smell, which is something that somehow never makes it into the abstract empire of the senseless. In the end, even a poet must eventually learn to prefer the real over the ideal, at least for a few hours out of the day. These poems are my boyfriend. He may dance funny, but he's mine.

—April, 2002

Notes on Performance and Staging

The subtitle of this book is *Poems, Stories and Monologues*, and I've tried to make sure that most pieces in the book are at least two of those three things.

One of the best things about Chicago's fringe performance scene is the sheer diversity of venues and audiences available to the writer-performer. In addition to a variety of stages for poetry reading and showcases for monologue work, there are plenty of free-form vehicles where writers can perfect a mutant, third-kingdom form of writing that blurs the boundaries between the two. Shows like *Too Much Light Makes the Baby Go Blind*, *The Pansy Kings' Cotillion*, Thax Douglas's *Thax After Dark*, *11 Minutes Max*, Scott Free's *Grinder* and many others allowed me to develop pieces that combine the musical and figurative qualities of poetry with the directness of prose, without stopping to worry about which side of the aisle the pieces would sit on if they had to choose.

This book is divided into three sections of poems (*What the Sea Means*, *Night Diaries* and *The Desires of Glass*) and one section of monologues and stories for the stage (*Big Glass Jar*). But for the reasons outlined above, the boundaries between those realms are far from cut and dried in my writing. Some of the pieces here were originally written for the reader's eye, and wound up finagling their way on stage in one show or another; others were written when I was on deadline for The Neo-Futurists or The Pansy Kings, but thematically they seem to belong with a certain group of poems from a certain period in time, so I've placed them there. Several of the pieces in *What The Sea Means* (the new chapbook of poems at the beginning of this collection) lean so far to the prose side of "prose-poem" that they challenge the elasticity of the term. But thematically they belong in the chapbook — in fact, they're essential to it, and its poetic argument would be incomplete without them.

I've chosen not to include stage directions in the actual texts of the performance pieces, partly in order to present them as streamlined, uncluttered texts for reading, and partly because some of them have been staged a number of different ways in different settings. But where appropriate, I've included descriptions of the pieces' stagings in the "Notes" section at the back of the book.

Finally, I should note that a number of the performance pieces in this book were accompanied on stage by music composed by and with the brilliant Alex Christoff, and the musicians from his various bands including King Spill and Snake Oil. Several of those pieces also featured video by my fellow Pansy King and frequent co-conspirator Kurt Heintz, or black-and-white film by Spin 1/2's resident filmmaker Armando Vasquez. The words stand on their own, but what my collaborators' music and images added to them was beyond words.

Performance and Publication History

From 1990-99 I was an active member of The Neo-Futurists theater company, writing and performing every week in their "30 Plays in 60 Minutes" late-night show *Too Much Light Makes the Baby Go Blind.* "The Idea of You," "Young Person's Guide to Synchronicity," and "Story #423" were previously published in *100 Neo-Futurist Plays from Too Much Light Makes the Baby Go Blind.* Those three pieces are also included in audio form on the 1997 *Too Much Light* CD. "A Trick of the Light," "The Buddha Receiving a Gift of Heart-Shaped Chocolates," "Jimmy, Roger & John," "Stonewalled, or The Sound of the Crowd," and "Talking to Myself" are also included in *Neo Solo: 131 Neo-Futurist Solo Plays from Too Much Light Makes the Baby Go Blind.* "Between the Lines in 4/4 Time," "Davy Jones in the Produce Department: A Piscean Parable," and "Stitching a Dummy" are also included in *200 More Neo-Futurist Plays from Too Much Light Makes the Baby Go Blind* (forthcoming as of this writing). In 1992 The Neo-Futurists produced *Blushing Under the Mushroom,* an evening of solo pieces by Lisa Buscani, Ayun Halliday, Greg Allen and myself. "The Buddha Receiving a Gift of Heart-Shaped Chocolates" and "Map of the Body" were first performed there.

In 1993 and '94 I produced and directed two shows under the auspices of a motley collective called Spin 1/2 Performance Conflux. "Staring at Orion's Left Foot," and the second part of "two poems appassionata" in slightly different form (under the title "The Sea Recedes Like Sleep"), were first performed in *The Collapsible Detachable Self-Cleaning Universe Show* ('93). "City Dream #8," "Parts of Me Function Like a Dream," "Please Drive Slowly," and "lughnassadh iii" were first performed in *Parts of Me Function Like a Dream* ('94).

In 1994 I founded The Pansy Kings, a collective of gay male performing artists. Our performance vehicles were *The Pansy Kings' Cotillion* ('94, '95 and '96) and *The Pansy Kings' Holiday Pageant* ('94 and '95). "Laughing Sal," "A Trick of the Light," "Told Me What?" "The Idea of You," "The Sea Recedes Like Sleep," and "Map of the Body" all turned up in the course of those performances.

The following pieces were included in my 1997 show *Talking to Myself*: "I ≠ AM," "Talking to Myself," "Big Glass Jar, or Pearls Go with Everything," "Snow," and "Talking to Myself: The Interview."

Acknowledgements

Profuse thanks are due to a number of people who provided editorial input on some or all of the material in this book. Genevra Gallo, Lisa Buscani, Ayun Halliday, David Alabach, and Corbin Collins all gave me diligent and detailed feedback; Rachel Claff, Donna Jagela, Karen Christopher, lynne Shotola, President Bob Stockfish, CJ Mitchell, Stephanie Shaw and Scott Hermes provided many helpful comments as well. (Special thanks to Scott for designing and proofreading the original Web publication of *Night Diaries*.) Thanks to Pierre Louveaux for emergency grammar consultation, Diana Slickman for OED word sleuthing and sundry other assistance, and Sandie Stravis for her amazing librarian powers.

I've already mentioned my multimedia collaborators Alex Christoff, Kurt Heintz and Armando Vasquez. Tim Clue, Timothy Buckley, Betsy Freytag and Karen Christopher all helped me with the process of staging *Talking to Myself*. Thanks are also due to all the members of the various performance groups I've worked with over the years, especially The Neo-Futurists, The Pansy Kings, and Spin 1/2. The ongoing collaboration I shared with them help shaped much of the material here.

Thanks to the various hosts and presenters who gave me opportunities to showcase my work, especially Sharon Korshak, Thax Douglas, Tim Anderson, Terry West and Paula Killen, Thom Jackobs, Live Bait Theatre, Paul Snagel and WZRD radio, Alan Amberg and LesBiGay Radio, Ira Glass, Eliz Meister and all at *This American Life*, Scott Free, Ann Christopherson and the staff at Women and Children First Books, and everyone at Unabridged Books.

Thanks to Cary Norsworthy, who took the Laughing Sal photo for the cover; to Kurt Heintz who stalked the "Please Drive Slowly" sign; to Jim Newberry, the paramedic photographer, for his great work over the years; and to Lori Dana, Kelly Clissold, Ken Willow, Allan Shiffrin and all at Image Studio for the book's beautiful design and cover.

Thanks to Gregg Shapiro, Christopher Stewart, Ellen Rosner, Yvonne Zipter, and David Irwin for encouragement at critical moments. I'm especially grateful to Diana Slickman, Lori Dana, Danielle Christoffel, lynne Shotola, Sandie Stravis, John Cavallino, Lisa Buscani, Tim Clue, Jeffrey Sculley and Kevin Spengel for friendship and support of the above-and-beyond variety; and to Dave Roberts, Kristine Hengl and all the Planet-Earthlings for the friendship and community that kept me going while compiling this book.

I want to thank my hosts, guides and companions for the travels I've written about in these pages: Russell Hoban, who helped me find my way to Glastonbury, Avebury and Stonehenge on my first visit to the UK; The Milton Keynesians, Les, Debbie and Jules, who made my first trip to Glastonbury especially memorable and who took me to the Rollright Stones the following summer; Ian Mitchell, who hosted me on the Isle of Lewis and patiently accompanied me as I sought out every tiny stone circle on the island; Corbin Collins and Tracy Brown, who took me on an all-day pilgrimage to the Dooncarton circle in Ireland; Kurt Heintz, my traveling companion for my first trip to the UK and Ireland; Anita Loomis, who sent me to visit the isle of Inchcolm; and Lydia Paweski and Chris Dodge, who hosted me on many trips to San Francisco to visit Laughing Sal. And a tip of the keyboard to Mike Scott of The Waterboys, for constant inspiration and some great travel tips, too — his music has been the soundtrack for my writing for the better part of two decades, as well as a travelogue for my own journeys.

Thanks to my family, especially my sister D. Jane, my mother Charlotte, and my roommate Dragon Lady for being there through the thick, the thin, and what's left when there's no more thin.

Finally, I wish to think my publisher and friend John Pierson, a.k.a Ian Pierce, Jughead, and all his other aliases and secret identities, for making this book possible.

What the Sea Means

Poems 1998-2002

A human being is a part of the whole, called by us "Universe," a part limited in time and space. He experiences himself, his thoughts and feelings, as something separated from the rest — a kind of optical delusion of his consciousness. This delusion is a kind of prison for us...
— Albert Einstein, from a letter dated 1950

Zeppo

All of your best moments took place offstage,
off the page, away from the cameras and the recorders.
Those who knew you knew what you were capable of,
but to the public you were only the rounder-out.
When you shone, it was for small and ephemeral
audiences, appreciative certainly, but posterity
was not among them.

Everyone always said that in person, you were much
funnier than the movies would allow.
Some even claimed that offstage, you were
the funniest of the four; but that's only hearsay now,
something to be quoted and noted in biographies
and memoirs. What we have are the films, where you
had to play it straight, a walking
cipher, a springboard for your brothers' antics.
The world thought of Arthur as the mute one,
but perhaps it was you who were silenced. There
was a justice in that perhaps — you hadn't paid the same
dues, hadn't grown up on the road. You got to
go to school, to live in a house rather than on a train.
But you also got left out of the story — or rather, say
that you were in your own story, not theirs, one
that existed for itself and not for the ages.
Where the frame stopped, that's where you began.
What showed up on celluloid was only your shadow.

It was your misfortune — or perhaps from another
perspective, your fortune — that your brilliance simply
occurred, without being preserved. Just like so many
other brilliant lives that were lived

without the attention of cameras and microphones,
with one difference: You turned up in the background
of the shot, and left a record of yourself to intrigue us.
Just an outline, just a sign: You stood at the edges
of the action, the ghost of yourself,
there to signify the larger part of life
cropped out by the borders of the frame.

The City Slept and Metal Phantoms

The city slept and metal phantoms sped along wooden tracks
through dark starless clusters of silent stone buildings.
Buses full of nocturnal creatures rattled north and south through
ghost town streets at long intervals.

The city yawned and stretched and coffeehouses opened
and its veins began to circulate with automobiles
and the carriers of goods.

The city thought of me and a pizza slid out
of a deep metal oven.
The city thought of you and a florist created a display
of red and gold Gerbera daisies.
The city thought of me thinking of you,
and a man slipped and fell on a patch of ice.

All day long millions of people swarmed here and there,
fulfilling the thoughts and desires of the city.
The city wore itself out with thinking and doing and
fighting and wanting and growing ever denser,
and its shops began to close.

Nervous, urgent residents of the city groped their way
around and into each other, in beds and living rooms
and cars and dark booths in video stores,
and the city trembled and subsided.
The eyelids of the city began to twitch and phantasms
were released into the streets of the city:
drag fairies in black tatters, club vampires in silver pants and
velvet capes, dreadlocks, gothic eyeshadow, purple mohawks,
piercings and baleful tattoos.

Now it is night again. Here and there, blood stains concrete
or carpet and the city gasps or jerks spastically in its bed.
Television signals crackle through its brain:
bankruptcy attorneys, phone sex vixens, trash talk shows,
sitcom reruns and all-night news. The city dreams helplessly
of Gomer Pyle and Hawkeye Pierce.

Tommy El

There are things I can say and things I can't,
things to be revealed and things more exciting
(and, strangely, available) when they are kept concealed —
and the challenge is to define you, invoke and circumscribe you,
without identifying or locating you,
without appearing to name you.
Writing a poem about you
without describing where and how
we met is like trying to write a novel
without the letter e. Even your name has two of them.
The Oulipists would say that these rules
are the constrictions that allow art to arise,
something to narrow the possible texts
that could be generated about you
down to a reasonable number.
These limitations are like the frame that bounds
(and thereby enables the existence of) a work of art,
the walls that create a home;
but perhaps the identifying details I must omit
are also something central that is missing, like the center hole
that defines a donut, distinguishes it from a mere lumpy cake.
The elided subject of this poem
is the place where certain fundamental necessities converge,
where attraction meets repulsion, danger becomes desire,
and it is kept hidden behind a veil because that flimsy barrier
both protects and arouses us. And so this poem is defined
by the curious void around which it orbits,
the fact that it never gets to the point, never homes in on
the terrible, exhilarating sweetness at the center of things.

The Flymaker Sweeps the Shop

At the first chill rattle of autumn's saber, I crawled out onto
the ledge and took up residence outside my own window.
I spent the morning spinning elaborate lies designed to ensnare
various other lies that were still cluttering up my
immediate environment; strangling each one in
sudden terminal threads as it came fluttering
or darting out of my writing space into the September chill,
blundering into the nearly-transparent lines and angles
of this year's last and greatest contrivance. And when my lies
were entangled like flies, I drank their sweet blackberry juices
and threw away the husks, growing fat and strong
for the coming winter, profiting from the way my fictions
and delusions had developed and complicated themselves
in response to the real world. (The phrase *real world* itself,
the moment I thought it, became ensnared in my web
and I quickly pinned it in silk, thrashing and struggling,
its blood bitter but quite satisfying.)

There is no housekeeper like a spider, none so neat and ruthless.
That unsparing arachnid sense of business is what's necessary
to rid the house of summer's flying creatures,
all those wings and glittering eyes stitched together
in fits of untempered poetic ecstasy:
moths and flies and June bugs hatched to circle
colored paper lanterns crazily in fits of batty passion,
flitter drunk on the odors of overripe fruit, drone or chirp
in the heat of pregnant yellow moonlight, soar on humid winds
and land footfirst on soft garden blossoms. Now I suck them dry,
deny and unmake them, destroy and betray them,
recycling their essences into something cold
and silent and crystalline, to survive the ice until

I can hatch them again — with no more chance
at long-term viability but perhaps
more vigor and daring, an extra flash of iridescence
in the wing, or a few more facets to the eye:
the conceits of a new year, toys to seduce the summer
while the winter's back is turned.

The New Planet

There are no fish kisses after midnight, no geraniums
howling in the window, no furry suns placing
their paws on your shoulders. But you can dig a tunnel anyway,
through the silver syrup of time, sugar down the throat
of benign memory, neutral potential.
I want to dance with you underneath the dance floor,
behind the walls of the music, where the lights can't see us.
I want to disarrange your hair tenderly in the men's room
while you talk about Bowie albums and the beat blares darkly
outside and occasionally the door opens letting in blasts of sound
and fabulous monsters who smile bemusedly
while your dark eyes watch me.

There are no fish kisses after midnight.
But there are silent sailing silver conveyances and a sky
with no rafters, and empty streets delicious with painted stripes
and abandoned newspapers and other blemishes
redolent of *sabi* and silence. My hearing returns slowly;
the cab could take me anywhere,
under the sea and over the moon, the streets glide away
beneath our wheels and I think of the sweat, the sound,
the door swinging open and then closed again.

What the Sea Means 2.0

As a child, you learn that
three-quarters of the earth's surface
is water. Everything that is not land is water,
and everything on the land depends on it.
Even your body is mostly water.
The water is you, and the water is inside you,
and everywhere you go, the sea is already there.
The sea is enormous, and it has no walls.
The sea is where you came from, the sea surrounds you,
the sea is incomprehensible yet it demands to be known;
and the sea is talking to you, all of the time,
trying to tell you something
in a language you can't quite understand.

No one can say what the sea means.
No one can mean what the sea says.

Plastic doll people sit in flimsy paper dollhouses
next to the roaring of the sea. They drink tea from tiny
plastic doll cups and pretend not to hear
the yammer and the howl of the sea outside.

When you were a child there was always the thought of the sea.
It was calm but ferocious, mysterious yet reassuring.
The thought of the sea was like a solitary child
walking along the edge of the actual sea
on a bright, clear day.

The thought of the sea had jellyfish in it,
but not the dead ones that float upside down, useless.

What does it mean to be free? What does it mean
to be able to go anywhere,
provided you have the craft and the energy?
What does it mean to look out over the vast, gelid sea
and have no thought arise?

The sea accosts you in frozen food aisles,
preventing you from reading lists of ingredients.
The sea repeatedly prevents you from catching your bus.

The sea resists all attempts to consolidate it,
organize it, alphabetize or prioritize it.
It spills out of drawers, tumbles off of book shelves,
litters the floors, cascades across the surfaces of desks
and tables. It calls you late at night and hangs up
after a moment of ponderous silence.

The sea sends you fourteen catalogs a week
and refuses to remove you from its mailing list.
It interrupts you when you're speaking,
and sidetracks you so you never find your way
back to the point you were trying to make.

When you were 19, the sea lived in the dorm room
upstairs from you. You would dawdle after meals
in the cafeteria, hoping it would come along and you could
attempt to initiate a conversation. Once, you caught sight of it
shirtless on the quad on a spring afternoon, and although the sea
is cool and made of water, the sight of it burned bright and
painful like the sun. You took to contemplating the moon and
avoiding the daylight in order to escape that burning glance.
In order to distract your hunger. You burned incense and
experimented with prayer to dead gods

and your skin turned pale like clouds
illuminated by the moon.

The sea keeps making obscene phone calls in which it suggests
that your problems are actually "opportunities."

The sea is a confidant who meets you at trattorias and cafés
and adopts a tone of almost vulgar familiarity when addressing
you, yet refuses to tell you its real name or where it lives
or what it really wants from you.

The sea already knows far too much about you
and you're not certain you can trust it,
in fact you're fairly certain you can't,
but you're in too deep to break things off now.

The sea distorts your reflection in mirrors
so you have no sense of your true shape.

The sea makes objects of all kinds appear much closer
than they are. It tells you that you need merely
stretch forth a hand to touch the clouds.

The sea can pick up the cat without getting scratched. The sea
cannot be created or destroyed. It expresses itself as both waves
and particles. Its behavior is always influenced by the presence
of the observer. Also, the sea looks much better in drag than you
do. The sea sometimes affects to refer to itself as The Ocean,
but it is, in fact, always the sea.

The sea masturbates outside your window at night
and shouts drunkenly.

When you were a child there was always the thought of the sea.
The thought of the sea is still there to comfort you,
but now sometimes you think you see the sea
standing behind the thought of the sea, rolling its eyes.

The sea wants you to know that this is all for your own good,
all debts eventually get paid and someone *is* keeping track and
this will all come out in the wash. Everything will matter when
the pieces are put away and the board is folded up, pristine,
silent, good as new. You have to take the sea's word for this.
The sea does not supply documentation.

But suppose the sea is right. Suppose the circle
is always closed when the journey is complete.
Will it matter to you then, when the game is over?
The sea won't say. In the meantime, you have work to do,
and the sea won't do it for you. The sea won't answer
your questions, you have to look them up
or work them out for yourself. That's how you learn.

The sea will occasionally rearrange the furniture,
just so you don't get too set in your ways.
The sea will occasionally flood your house, to remind you
that you have no possessions. And if you try to stay in one place,
the sea will swallow you up, to remind you that in the sea there
are no places, there is only endless horizon,
and infinite water, and borders and boundaries are just illusions.
Then the sea will cough you up on dry land to remind you
that you do not have power over these illusions, just yet,
and yes, you can get hurt.

Better start walking, the sea says.
You have a long way to go, and there are birds in the sky that

want to eat your eggs as soon as you lay them
in the sand, and there is no packing up before the game is over.
You are in it, and if you don't play it you are not *not* playing it,
you are merely playing it poorly.

No one can say what the sea means.
No one can mean what the sea says.
But you must listen, and listen, and scratch your head.
And you must paddle and keep paddling,
and you cannot stop paddling in order to listen.
You must open the mail the sea sends you and
pick up the phone when it calls.
Attempts at evasion will only cost you time.

When you were a child you thought of the sea,
and now you think of your thoughts of the sea,
and it all seems so far away;
but that only means that you are in the sea,
not on dry land looking out at the horizon
but in the actual sea; and the thought of the sea
is the sea, and the sea is in you and the sea is you.
And you walk along the edge of the thought of the sea
like a child, picking its way carefully
among the rocks and the algae,
and the thought of the sea thinks of you,
and it smiles.

Night Passage Home

Rhythm of tender leaves
tracing their patterns of shadow on faces and
sidewalks under the Midsummer
moon which looms, waiting for the next
breath. Cats hide panic-eyed in the
gardens and grasses behind the gates
you pass, watching your footsteps
go by, agents of the moon, in league
with the fireflies. The entire night
communicates with itself using
a soft and rustling code,
semaphore, signals, whisper and nudge,
sharing a vast interconnected gentlemen's
agreement which surrounds you but does
not quite include you, except to the
extent that it tolerates you passing
through it, like a magic forest that
guides travelers through its depths:
unharmed, unshaken except for
certain sudden glimpses of the
eldritch monstrosities that it shelters
(for the most part of its days)
from human sight — and with whom,
for just the briefest of moments,
you lock eyes; just long enough
to carry the broken fire of their gaze
away with you, to trouble
the ocean of your summer dreams.

The City You Almost Lived In

The city you almost lived in is going about its life without you. Its buses charge up and down its crowded streets, with one empty seat, and from time to time the driver starts as if he's heard someone pull the bell, when in fact nobody has. People on the sidewalks occasionally part as if to let someone through. There's a 24-hour diner with one table in the corner where (on certain nights of the week) nobody ever seems to be sitting between the hours of one and three a.m. There's a loose semicircle of friends, people who genuinely like each other and want to spend more time together, but who can never quite manage to organize social events that bring them all together in a satisfying way. And there's a humble but decent apartment in a mildly bohemian neighborhood, with plenty of windows, relatively modern appliances and a nice back porch where someone could sit with a cup of peppermint tea and watch the sky while gradually waking up — but for some reason the landlord can never keep it occupied for long, despite the housing shortage. There's a scrawny orange tabby that lives in the alley behind the building, and while it allows a consortium of neighbors to collectively feed it, it attaches itself to none of them as primary human. Just a few blocks away, the lover you haven't met is getting ready for bed, a little depressed tonight, because some curious and elusive center seems to be missing, like an idea that wants to be realized and articulated but instead lurks just behind an invisible membrane.

Meanwhile, in the city where you live, a thousand miles away, you go through the motions of your days feeling increasingly off-kilter, like when you used to stay home from school and you knew that the day you were supposed to be having was going ahead without you, and there was the discomforting sense of certain possibilities being deducted from the account of your life. You sometimes dream of an airport where baggage sits unclaimed, while you ride home in a cab with an empty trunk. You sit up in bed with the panicked sense that it's now days later, and you're only now realizing what you've forgotten, what is now certainly long gone.

At the end of the day, some days, you sit at your desk and look out the window that faces west, and occasionally feel that the desk, the walls, the ceiling and everything around you are becoming pale and insubstantial, as if you could see through them into some other life that made more sense. And you pause and put your chin in your hand, and you clear your mind as if to allow something you can't quite sense to come into it, and the only thing that does is the odd sense that at this very moment, somebody somewhere is doing the exact same thing.

Letter to Mark in Dublin

Most of the time I can barely stand my own company,
let alone anyone else's. But that last night in Dublin,
having journeyed around the world to sneak
in the back door of my own seventh house, the night
seemed made of connection, the stars dots
just begging for a pencil. So when I found you
at my side in a basement pub, silly and sensitive,
vulnerable and needing to talk,
smiling across the bar at my American accent and then
slowly edging your way to my elbow,
full of that courtly rising and falling nonsense
that flows through the heart of Dublin like the Liffey itself,
I knew all I had to do was listen to you long enough
and you'd follow me outside; and then I followed you
through the dirty good-natured streets where as always
lovers paused in pairs occupying every available doorway,
sheltered under sculpture and signposts, anywhere really,
and kissed as if the world were ending and there were
nowhere else to go. I followed and adored you as you
made fun of your own foolishness,
apologizing sheepishly for the bewilderment
that made you so intoxicating.
Telling me the jokes you stored up to impress the tourists,
some of them two or three times,
rippling along in that single unceasing sentence
that only Joyce could fully capture,
and the stream only stopped once, for a moment as we kissed
on the O'Connell Street bridge
under the watchful eyes of the patriots, the poets,
and the river-goddess herself.

And then I understood the problem of the
lovers in doorways, the ones
I'd been watching for a week now, wondering why
they lingered on street corners with nowhere to go.
In the States we take it for granted: private rooms
cheap and plentiful, no questions asked,
believing freedom our birthright.
But in other places there are always watchful eyes.
You had a problematic roommate, I had a somewhat
more problematic and rather frightening doorman
to contend with, cross between a small-town sheriff
and a Dickens headmaster, meaning
no room at the inn, no safe and
decent place for us to discover each other.

And so I followed again as you led me through
the impossibly empty streets, a dark purple
watercolor of a narrow European avenue,
shadowy under an electric moon, not a single
light in any window. You were a little
afraid of where you were taking me, the unmarked
doorway, the filthy stairs, and that made us both
a little more excited and I remember you
trembling as I undressed you in the locker room,
then splashing under the cold water
in the shower room,
naked and lopsided and dirty,
and I knew I'd arrived in my own
perfect foreign film moment, complete with
a raggle-taggle Irish boy, a self-described
"skinny git" who only stopped talking long enough
to kiss me, still trembling as we embraced
but laughing, too,

as we held each other in the water
and the rising steam.

It was my last night in Dublin and neither of us
was disappointed by it, not even disappointed
when it was over and we were chased back out into the street.
Our night together was like a sign you glimpse
through the window of a hurtling train: You know
there isn't time to read all of it so you grope
for a few key words to cling to, and try to assemble
meaning and structure from them later, in private.
I came here to observe details knowing that I would forget
most of them, but you're the impression that survives,
your outlines deepening even as the detail wears away.

We knew our time was short and we weren't bothered by it,
because time can be stretched out thin and flimsy
or compressed into something more urgent, more
substantial, a moment that endures precisely
because it's packed so small and tight with awareness,
like the dense flesh of a white dwarf star.
And besides, I was fairly sure there'd be a poem in it, or maybe
a dozen if I made the story last, took it apart slowly,
looked at it piece by piece. So I didn't panic when you
gave me that last clumsy embrace on the sidewalk,
a final shabby crooked grin, and then ambled away
into the slowly brightening morning,
following the river back into the city,
to sleep at the base of its stream of language,
the place where its watery rocking
generates the rhythm of its discourse.

The Sentence Suspended

There are words and words and words and just as the sentence begins to despair the end suddenly looms and the period arrives. And the sentence is allowed to disappear into that small round black perfection, its endless rooms furnished with luxurious oblivion, during which time stops. Soon (in the temporal sense of the larger paragraph) the sentence will have to emerge from its rabbit hole and be reborn as the next sentence, regaining its momentum so that the paragraph can continue toward its own Lethe, the synapse or indentation before the next paragraph. But for the moment, inside the sanctuary of the period, the sentence's pyramid, no time passes, or else it passes so slowly as to seem irrelevant. The sentence takes off its boots, has a cup of steaming cider, looks aimlessly out the window at the clumps of nearby letters which seem random and nonsensical from this vantage point. And it thinks about the many texts it has snaked its way through, and the many still to come, and wonders what they all mean, when you average them all out. And what it means that from a few simple components, sooner or later everything is said, all texts created, all positions asserted and argued. And at the end, it wonders, will anything have been said, or will the fact that everything was said mean that nothing was said, that in fact there was nothing to be said? Or is it possible that one word will emerge from the smoke and the rubble to stand apart from the rest, one word that could not be balanced or cancelled out by anything else, one word that will be revealed at the end of time and language as the one true word spoken by the universe? And a small bell rings and the sentence knows that it must emerge from its pyramid, its period, and allow what must happen to happen, the beginning to end and the end to begin. And in the space between the moment the period's door slams shut behind the exiting sentence and the first dramatic glimpse of the incoming capital letter, a weight descends, a burden is lifted, and everything is forgotten, and the sentence is relieved of its sentience, no longer sentenced to sense: It is oblivious even to oblivion, and it is one with the one true word as the world draws its breath and in the next moment the world is speaking again in the way that it will and the sentence continues anew, reborn, blithely talking like a chattering child on its way to school and a new wide-eyed life, having forgotten everything it knows about not knowing; newly minted and ignorant enough to attempt to make a true statement about something or something else, a chutzpah that will delight and appall it when it arrives once again at that perfect circle of peace in the place between its lives.

Moth Song for a New Summer

The window is shut like the
answerless death of god
and the sill is littered with dust and the shells
of other fliers. I am trapped here but
not by the design or intention of any intelligence;
this barrier so finally arbitrary, unnecessary.
Let me go through that doorway into the silence
that will unmake me. Let me lay aside the
frets and the frame, the strings and the
struggle, and let me do it painlessly,
suddenly, whisking out
through the momentarily opened window
into a blinding daylight that swallows, forgets,
embraces, absolves. All space is pain, all time
is separation, all identity is confusion,
all doors are walls, all light is silence.
In movement we forget, in stillness we
pay the interest that has accrued during our distraction.
There is no way to avoid the approaching collision
except to circumvent the circumstances that
impose it. Open the window. I will not move
until you do.

Alas, Hyacinth

Alas, poor Hyacinthus is dead. Worse, he did not
die by Apollo's hand; no discus was thrown, for
Apollo stood him up. Zephyrus, that tired old queen,
couldn't so much as summon a gust. The sun-god and his
beautiful crowd had other blossoms to pluck, stayed
up all night reveling on Olympus,
where only the fairest may ascend.
And Zephyr, by his nature, isn't interested unless
Apollo is interested: What doesn't require stealing
isn't worth having. And so Hyacinth died, not
cut down in a blaze of beauty and jealous desire; rather,
say he faded unobserved, like a flower pressed
between the pages of a book, deprived of sun and air.

No flowers mark his passing,
no cries of "AI AI, AI AI":
Hyacinth is dead, and because
no gods fought for him, he will not be pitied,
nor poeticized, nor planted in suburban flower beds
to live again in the springtime.
The stories do not lie, in general; but neither do they always
specifically apply. Some stories pass you by, like the flight
of birds — beautiful, unattainable, a motion that seems to
belong to all but which in fact is reserved for the few.

Mourn for Hyacinth, who was not beautiful,
and will be forgotten.
And who nonetheless has passed, nonetheless lay bleeding,
nonetheless was once young, and is no more.

Critique of the Geometrical State

Defined by an arbitrary geometry,
circumscribed by an inexplicable skin.
Trapped in a hostile topology;
prisoner of unasked-for points, lines, arcs.
The lungs expand and contract
like insane circus balloons. The fists
clench and unclench, the eyes roll back and forth,
while the second hand clicks through its orbit.
You are like a light moving in a closed room
searching the walls, the ceiling, the floor,
for any means of entrance or egress;
baffled, confounded, its existence absurd,
trapped in a state of being with no source and no terminus.
You review the things you are aware of:
The sun is round, earth's orbit an ellipse.
Light, a gradient, shades up from the horizon
at sunset; birds puncture the deep flat background,
holes poked in the lid of a jam jar full of fireflies,
pepper scattered across a bowl of soup.
The house rectangular, its peaked roof triangular,
windows crisscrossed into four-ups,
lines, angles, everything in its place.
The body irregular, three-dimensional,
uncalled-for; no receipt, no return.
It's a joke that no one gets
because the form is awkward, unbalanced,
inward grace obscured by drab packaging.

Like a moth's angry wings battering
the glass of its transparent prison,
you take a compass and draw perfect

circle after perfect circle on a sheet of paper
with one ragged edge. The circles become
portholes into infinite ground without figure,
a field of light without shadow,
music without measure, being without dimension:
The light escapes its windowless box and
the shapeless joke expands until it dwarfs perception,
which resembles a shelled peanut in orbit around the sun.
Geometry's traffic cops write no tickets here,
for they may not go where their shadows cannot follow.
There is no box, there is no light,
no circles, no lines, no points, no arcs.
There will be a bill to pay in the morning;
but for now the Ouroboros guards the door.
Back on earth, time continues to pass:
Children look up at the sky
and feel they are falling.

Safe from the Moon

We go for a stroll on an August night
and try to ignore the disturbing

sounds the moon is making. Why is he so
intent on destroying our evening?

We have made friends with every thing,
even the shadows, but the moon insists

on obstructing our path with upsetting odors,
hostile dogs, sticky substances, frightening personages,

appalling and terrible insects. Now we only want
to get home, but the moon, that bully, leads us on

a horrified trek through alleys and brambles,
parking lots glittered with shards of glass,

churchyards gashed with freshly-turned earth.
Lost, we are lost, and we cannot believe

that once we were in love with the moon.
We must choose our heroes

more carefully, we must not get in the car
with strangers, we must not think the world

is more friendly than it is. If we ever
make it home again, we will shut the moon

out, with iron and crosses, smudge-stick
and garlic, not let that fat face peer in at us again;

live out our lives unloved, alone, but safe at last,
safe from the moon at last.

Watching Him Dance

Despite all attempts at diversion toward the edges,
we are drawn toward the center where the activity is.
Despite our best attempts to lurk in the shadows at the fringe,
it is impossible not to look toward the center,
not to follow you there, though we cannot enter,
cannot be there with you. Somehow it seems enough to keep
the center in view. Somehow it seems enough not
to be banished somewhere out of sight, to know that
if things were different, yes, if things were different.
And the difference would be slight, and the space that must
be crossed not so vast after all. And we hover on the brink of that
realization and then go skating away, before things become too
intense, and we say things that might destroy that fine balance
that allows us to come here at all. It's amazing what you can hold
in your hands as long as you make no sudden moves,
don't confuse proximity with possession,
don't attempt to touch the image
in the water: just regard the center
with a calm, still gaze.

Glastonbury
(*for Debbie, Les and Jules*)

Eerie, like something from an alien landscape,
three moons in the sky or a double sun,
to remind you that you have left your earth
behind, that you are in the universe of story now —
eldritch, that mystic green hill with its crazy ruined tower
is always above, behind you,
wherever you go in this town
it follows you like the moon,
shrouded in mist or beaming in bright afternoon sunlight
while the buskers and the tourists and the card shops
go about their business.

The climb up the height nearly killed me, huffing and sweating
while goth girls with Teletubby backpacks ran giggling ahead.
But worth it on a grey day, to stand on the Tor as the winds
come up and the children shriek and a tingle runs up your spine
as you think that this is the place, where
the lost stories behind the stories played out,
movies made without cameras to violate their secret dignity.

Even the approach is dramatic, at least for a Chicagoan abroad,
on board the Badgerline bus from Bristol;
armed with a backpack full of Waterboys discs, and a Discman
playing "The Return of Pan" to make the mood. These
professional-looking English crows, cows with their backs
to the road, blazing buttercups, all seeming knit together
in conspiracy. Through stony tunnels and stands of mossy trees,
following that dotted line up hill and down
until the gasp and the sudden, foolish tears
when the Tor appears small and distant, green-grey,
like a special effect in a fantasy film.

And the town with its camera stores and cheese shops,
and the people who live there — Have they become immune?
Is there a tolerance for this ambience? — going about their
Friday business; and the tourist maps that guide you
to the associated wonders:
the ruined cathedral melting into slabs like a Dali painting,
surreal in sudden showers with the sun still burning; and the
reputed graves of Arthur and Guinevere, a place where
stories are buried if not actual bodies; the well in the garden,
nestled silent among the blossoms, its summer air
thick with the synchronicity that turns chance meetings
into fateful friendships;
and the meditative thorn tree, hermit of Wearyall Hill —
perhaps some descendent
of Joseph of Arimathea's thorn, perhaps not,
but striking in its crooked dignity nonetheless,
gazing hill to hill with the tower on the Tor, its mystery
well-guarded by its throng of acolyte cows who seem
to take their job as caretaker seriously,
surrounding it with a deadly cowpie minefield, and
massing on the muddy path to glare
and scrutinize each comer who dares to approach
the solitude of its height.

Glastonbury, there was a time when the waters gathered
at your feet, when you rose out of the lake like a revelation;
the metaphysical throb of you brought clerics and mages to
study, poets and pilgrims from distant lands,
and the druid choirs enchanted you
night and day with songs that still charge
the air and the soil of you.
Now the waters of another time have receded, and
you are surrounded by a patchwork of fields instead;

360 degrees of green and grain, trees and dry roads that lead
to the distances of another world, where time has traveled on.
But the half-life of your legend is nowhere in sight, the density
of history and fable still felt in your gravitational pull.

And on a wild, windy afternoon, the average American tourist,
on what should be an average Friday,
can believe for a moment that he is Merlin,
gazing into the grey distance for a glimmer of what will be.

Dancing with Otto
(for the Earthlings)

Each week a window opens, a square of motion
and colliding energies in which
decorated molecules scheme and swarm,
and among them you and I.
It's a curious space, in which
spasms of grace are bounded by
scattered reflections of light.
The room seems to revolve and although
the evening must begin and end at some point,
from the vantage point of the foci
it is a vast, flashing ellipse without origin or terminus.
We hardly notice how the crowd floods and ebbs
around us as the hours pass like a procession
of ripe, pregnant moons. The magician
in his high tower performs his incantations and signs
for us, only for us, and the flashing silver regalia
of his order is set into its complicated motion
at our behest.

A Perfectly Empty Room

He kept dreaming of a perfectly empty room. He would spend all day carrying things out of his apartment, hauling them downstairs to the trash, trying to create a perfectly empty space; but somehow he awoke every day surrounded again by things. At night objects would infiltrate and colonize his home. Chairs would crawl in through open windows like wooden spiders, bookcases and potted plants would climb up the trellis, books and CDs would waft under the door as steam and reassume their shapes once inside, forming stacks and piles on tables, the floor, anywhere.

And each day he'd repeat the task of hauling his possessions down the back stairs to the garbage bin. It would take him hours to clear everything out. He worked at it single-mindedly, like an ant, with the image of bare walls and an open, sunlit expanse of floor in his mind. He discovered that old photographs — the hardest things to part with, except for the books — only exerted their pull on him while he was looking at them, but once they were gone he never thought of them again. He packed things up and carried them away with an attempt at blind detachment, forcing himself not to sort, examine or linger over the cargo as it passed through his hands on the way out of his life.

But even on those rare occasions when he managed to temporarily clear his room of real objects, he found it still crowded with the ideas of objects. There would be the translucent outline of a bookcase against the wall, the exact dimensions of a table in the center of a room. He would stumble over the place where a chair might be, knock over stacks of the absence of books. In the afternoon he'd catch himself pouring water on the windowsill to nurture nonexistent plants, gazing at a patch of unevenly faded paint on the wall that suggested a painting of a cypress tree on a hillside.

He could never empty his room. There was no emptiness around him, and not enough inside him to serve as antidote to the chaos of his surroundings. There wasn't enough void in the world to clear it all away. He could form a bucket brigade, ask his friends to help pass him pail after pail of nothing, flooding his apartment with absence and void, and still things would appear faster than he could wash them away. Sometimes it seemed that his possessions rose into the air and whirled around him, taunting him, taking on faces and expressions like a scene from an animated Disney film.

Why must everything be so present? he wondered. In a universe that is supposed to be mostly void, why do I only see things, everywhere I look? How does being create the illusion of outpacing emptiness, when the uncreated so outnumbers the created? And then he thought of the millions and billions of uncreated, nonexistent things that were inside him, around him, above him in the heavens and below him in the earth. And he knew that despite his present state of being, ultimately he was one of those uncreated, nonexistent things. He knew that he was only the possibility of himself, and the moment in which atoms appeared to arrange themselves to give him an outline was itself only one of many possibilities, none of them less real than any other, no less real than a song when no orchestra is playing it. An orchestra of molecules was playing the song of his being, and when they finished, the musicians would go home to their dinners and beds and forget about him, and eventually they would play other compositions, other themes. He would be unbodied, invisible, intangible, an idea that would haunt the cluttered space of someone else: some other bodied melody, frustrated in its quest for silence.

Bestiary

Airplane

For centuries, no winged creature would help
humans defy that line drawn by the gods between
earth and sky. A human could rise no higher
than a mountain would consent to let him climb;
even the rare winged horse
would buck a rider who aspired to violate
heaven's restraining order.
Till one day the airplanes arrived,
a sleek army of them shining like Prometheus,
and knelt on concrete runways, allowing
the marveling humans to mount and ride them
up; did they know they would destroy heaven
and replace it with clouds?
No one knows what penalty
the gods exacted for the violation of their law;
some fear the punishment is that there isn't any.

America

The America is known primarily for its thick, sticky,
brownish secretions, which distinguish it from
certain other wild landmasses and nation-states you
might encounter in the wild, (e.g. *Europe*, *Africa*,
or *Canada*). If you see an America coming toward
you in the forest, it is important not to provoke it.
You will be expected to lap up some of the secretions,
which are called *Coca-Cola*, and pretend that you
like them. After a while, you may come to believe
that you do, particularly if the America subjects you to
its *television*. It is now that the America is at its most

dangerous and most seductive; there is no known
antidote to the secretions, except for certain political
philosophies which can be toxic in their own right
if applied with excessive vigor; worse, to an America,
most of them smell like prey. Most importantly, do not
come between the America and its supply
of *petroleum* (the raw material it consumes,
digests, and secretes as Coca-Cola). It will interpret
any interference with its access to petroleum as a threat
to its offspring, and it will devour yours
as a prophylactic measure.

Automobile

The automobile is the dream beast of contemporary
Western civilization. It is seen charging out of
mist and fog, up and down mountains
while ethereal voices keen. It is the Helen
for which the *America* (q.v.) goes to war.
It is the Moloch to whom we write
blank checks of sacrifice. It is possible
to learn to travel without it; but your speech
will become unintelligible
to most of the people you meet.

Banjo

The distinctive "plinking and jangling"
cry of the banjo serves it well on a number of
fronts: It repels the banjo's natural enemies,
while drawing to it various easily manipulated
creatures who will aggressively handle its
stamen and pistils, becoming infected with its music
and thus carrying away the spores of the idea *banjo*

to various factories and craftsmen, where it will
interact with their hands and machinery to replicate
others of its kind. Do not be taken in by
its calculated air of comic humility. The banjo
will eat your grandmother for an afternoon's entertainment.

Bed

The bed is a large, amphibious creature
that waits on the shores of dry land for people
to come along, and lures them into its soft,
inviting interior. Once it has secured its prey,
it lumbers off, carrying them back to the
somnolent oceans, there to nourish itself with the rich,
salty dreams they produce, as they are gradually soaked
in the rhythmically lapping waters of its habitat.

Cafeteria

How children and poets alike
adore the cafeteria, for the beauty and whimsy
it embodies. Its elegant plumage and striking decorations
defy biological explanation, seem to serve no purpose other
than to introduce beauty into the world: the crumbling
slices of pie, the congealing soups, the tiny marshmallows
wobbling upon gelatin, the thick, lumpy substances
in serving vats, the coffee stirrers and the plastic trays and the
oyster crackers sealed in plastic. Whoever denies
that the Creator was an artist and a poet
has never encountered that luxurious beast, *cafeteria*.

Dresser

The dresser ensures its survival
by making itself useful to humans, who each insist

on having one or more of them around. The human keeper
opens each of the various mouths of the dresser (some species
have more than a dozen!) and inserts a wide variety
of foodstuffs — including but not limited to
items of clothing, jewelry, diaries, sexual playthings
and prophylactics, documents and photographs —
which remain in the dresser's mouths for periods ranging from
hours to decades, while the dresser slowly digests the notion
of the objects, the weight and the shape
and the folds and creases of them.
Eventually the humans will return to remove the digested
husks of the objects, temporarily or permanently:
not realizing how they have fed the dresser,
never noticing the loss of the nutrition that has been taken,
or if they do, putting it down casually to time and wear.

Encyclopaedia

The various microorganisms that are classed
under the heading *encyclopaedia* used to primarily
infect large printed hardcover volumes, and propagated
themselves through the agency of neatly-dressed
gentlemen carriers who knocked on the doors
of well-groomed suburban homes,
there to gently persuade the occupants
that they should provide encyclopaedia
with suitable habitat and care. Over the last
several decades, however, encyclopaedia have
evolved rapidly and are now capable
of disseminating themselves as streams of pure data
flashing across wires connected to computers.
They are generally regarded
as beneficial, even desirable organisms,
like the flora in yogurt or miso.

Still, their rapid development and the increasing ease
with which they are communicated
may be cause for attention.

Flashlight

The flashlight is an undependable creature —
his remarkable night vision can be a boon
to others in a wide variety of circumstances,
yet he is likely to let you down on precisely
those occasions when his clear vision is needed,
due to depleted energy or a sudden need for surgery
on his single, delicate eye. Though a symbol of clarity,
he is all too often a mere accomplice to obscurity.

Garbanzo Bean

The larval form of the *falafel* and the *hummus*.
For many years garbanzo beans got no respect,
because they were beige and therefore
assumed to be dull. Eventually a plurality of
the garbanzo beans hired a consultant and
rebranded themselves as *chickpeas*, at which point
they were discovered and made newly chic
by lesbians and other cutting-edge foodists,
and now they are always invited
to the best parties. They can frequently
be found in close proximity to
pita bread, in which they tend to nest.

Harlequin

The harlequin is not to be spoken of
in polite company.

Icicle

The icicle hangs like a bat from your eaves,
gleaming in the cold sunlight, thinking frozen thoughts,
aiming itself at the ground like a crystal dart.
Though it is a creature of winter,
a warm spring day will move it to tears.

Isosceles Triangle

The isosceles triangle is one of
the more pernicious agricultural pests.
It is prone to trampling crops
with its flat base, and capable of
wounding both humans and farm animals
with its vicious point. In addition,
isosceles triangles have been known
to infest granaries, quarter themselves
in peasants' huts, drink all the brandy,
and occasionally carry off fair young maidens.
So far no effective pesticides have been developed
to keep the isosceles triangles in check; fortunately
they don't breed very rapidly, due to lack
of applicable apparatus.

Jar

You swallow but you never digest, jar,
you contain but you cannot conceal;
you are only your hunger which
cannot ever be satisfied
even when you are fed,
and the shameful objects of your
frustrated appetites
are laid naked for the world to see.

Knife

The knife lies quietly in the kitchen drawer,
its one long tooth extended, dreaming of vegetables,
bread, flesh, anything: the moment
when it is drawn from its secret rubber tray
like sword from scabbard, when it flashes in the light
to sever and stab, keen and clever,
feeding on the merciless separation
of tissue from tissue, triumphantly rending
soft puny matter, which is doomed to part
before its irresistible assertion of will:
cleaving thing from thing,
making multiplicity from unity, feeling no remorse
for the division that follows in its wake.
The knife has no space in its carnivorous wit
with which to imagine the desolation
of the formerly whole made incomplete
by its passage: It was born to understand
only the slashing dandy joy of the deep slice,
the satisfaction of its thirst for cutting slaked,
before returning again to its long serrated sleep.

Lamp

Though it is the source of all light in the room,
the lamp hides its brilliance behind a shade,
stands back in the corner so as not to draw
attention to itself as it illuminates others,
makes them glow with its own donated radiance.
If you were watching a film about the lamp,
you would be moved to shed a tear for its
humility, its selfless service to others,
the lack of thanks and credit it gets

for the glory it lends to others.
As it is you are likely, if you think about it
at all, to notice that it is a bit ugly,
could certainly be replaced.

Macaroon

Macaroon, macaroon;
that exotic coconut fish of the candy counter
and the bakery window; how it swims through
our dreams. How we crave the sweetness of it
on winter afternoons, dipped in chocolate at a café
or on a rainy autumn evening
in front of the television. Its proprietary genius
is to strike a paradoxical balance
between the exotic and the familiar,
hinting of a tropical wildness that does not become unruly,
somehow simultaneously exciting and comforting.
You will find the macaroon strangely endearing;
its sweetness will slip beneath your defenses
to become your heart's companion, always there for you,
so easy to trust and to rely upon. To say that it is only
a cookie is to say the Sistine Chapel
is only a room in a church, Shakespeare's sonnets
a collection of mash notes, Lassie a mere trained dog.
You may fail to appreciate the virtues of the macaroon,
I suppose, but if you are such a philistine I suggest you do not
announce it in my presence, or I may be forced
to defend the honor of the macaroon. Then again,
perhaps it is well to remember
that separation from the macaroon is its own
terrible punishment, and those who inflict
such a fate on themselves deserve mainly
our compassion.

Necktie

An oddly shaped creature
worn by many as a form of ornamentation:
for some a badge of status and style,
for others a mark of servitude. There is much
lore and disagreement about the behavior
of the necktie; little is known for sure.
Some accuse the necktie
of subtly strangling its host —
gradually, so gradually that the prey never
knows it is being killed. Others see the necktie's
relationship to the human as a fashionable mark
of grace, like a butterfly's decision to light
on one's nose. Still others have suggested
that much depends on whether the tie is fat
or skinny, hungry or sated when first encountered,
and whether worn by day at the office, or by night
at the clubs. More research is needed; however,
I would prefer that others conduct it.

Offspring

Unlike the Kenneth Rexroth Bestiary
that inspired them, these poems were not
particularly written
for anyone's children.

Puddle

The puddle is a mystical,
meditative beast: Apparently
unconcerned with hunting,
mating or acquiring territory,
it spends its brief life

in reflection,
reflecting upon the sky, the branches of
trees that surround it, the faces of passers-by
peering down —
and all the while it gradually
sublimes, evanescing into pure spirit,
leaving nothing behind
when it's gone, no earthly baggage
or scores to be settled.
Monks and hermits would do well
to study the puddle; it seems likely
that many of the better ones
have done so.

Q

The Q is exotic, and exciting,
considered a little dangerous and perverse.
It makes most people uncomfortable
and they prefer not to look at it too
closely. Most people never attempt
to hold a direct conversation with it, and
are too shy to ask the librarian for the book
about it (which is kept behind the desk).
The Q is native only to one small
South Sea island, where the
customs are very different and visitors
seldom come. But the Q moves among us
in our own lands, and it is capable
of implanting a wild suggestion in our heads
from time to time; and we surprise ourselves
by visiting that strange island in the middle
of some otherwise ordinary day.

Raisin

Raisins? Do not speak to me
of raisins. The raisin is a bad joke,
an affront. If you want to know what
it is, I will tell you: A raisin is nothing
but a prune made out of a grape.
It exists mainly to spoil oatmeal cookies.
Enough. We should talk about
something else, before I
get too angry.

Shoe

Before you were born, your shoe was there,
waiting for your foot to fill it. Your
shoe walked back and forth across the earth,
mapping the journeys the two of you would
make together. But imagine if things had turned out
differently — suppose it wasn't your shoe at all,
but instead was bought and worn by somebody else?
Would your foot miss the shoe, know something was wrong,
feel uncomfortable in all the shoes it actually wore?
And would it know to grieve for those journeys,
travels that belonged to it in another life, but upon which
— in this one — it would never embark?

Tea Kettle

No one can properly articulate
the sadness of the tea kettle.

Trousers

The anaconda must unhinge its jaw
in order to devour a human whole;

the *trousers* need only a top button undone
and a zipper pulled down (unless the human
has recently gained some weight). But
a pair of trousers can never swallow more than
half a person; for the rest of the day
it walks around with its breakfast
hanging out of its mouth. Fortunately,
no one notices. The trousers' strategy
has been successfully adopted by a variety
of other creatures, including *corporations*
and *political parties*: If you must devour your prey
in public, try to make it look as if you are performing
a valuable service to humanity.

Umbrella

Psychics have sometimes
confused the umbrella
with a snake crawling out of a hole;
books and movies have suggested that umbrellas
give certain magical nannies
the power of flight.
For the earthbound, however,
it is most generally prized
as a means of protection
from the larval form of the species *puddle* (which see).
Although the umbrella gets its name
from the Latin word for shadow,
if you carry one for shade
on a hot summer day
you will likely be vexed by many
unfortunate attempts at wit.

Violin

The violin and its more domestic
cousin, the fiddle, are nearly
indistinguishable, except that the fiddle
is generally in a better mood. They are kept
as pets by both the cultured
and the bucolic.
The singing of the violin
can lure monsters into your
parlor, and calm their madness:
but do not get so cozy with them
as to offer a cigar.

Wednesday

Wednesday is generally innocuous
and docile, though somewhat given
to melancholy. However, if
you annoy Wednesday to the point where it becomes
seriously ruffled, it will surprise you with its capacity
for violence and outré behavior. In general,
Wednesday should be given a wide berth
and not provoked.

X-Ray

The x-ray is a speed-of-light
peeping tom. It seeks
only to learn your secrets,
and then it abandons
you, as if the blinding flash
of intimacy you shared
were nothing to it.
It penetrates your flesh easily, too

easily, and in an instant it knows
more about you than
you know about yourself:
what your skeleton looks like
under your skin, where the fracture
lies, what's developing
inside your lungs. This radioactive
intimacy can't last long,
and the x-ray is gone from your life
almost the very moment
it has you all figured out.
And the only evidence of its
voyeuristic passage through your life
is the information it leaves behind,
the fact that you're a little wiser now.

Yo-Yo

The yo-yo is one of the animal kingdom's
comedians, a ruthless practical joker.
It seeks out a susceptible human
who quickly becomes
attached to it. The human believes
that it "owns" the yo-yo and
is "training" it, and all the while
the yo-yo is gleefully
conditioning the human to
humiliate itself in public with a series of
bizarre gestures and arm waving,
idiotic repetitive motions. In rare
cases this may even be televised.
The yo-yo secretly finds it all
hilarious, and that nasty
satisfaction is the yo-yo's nourishment.

However, if the yo-yo should happen
to take a liking to you,
it will spare you these indignities
by allowing you to think
that you are simply
bad with a yo-yo.

Zero

Round and perfectly
smooth as an egg,
and just as pregnant with possibility,
this elusive creature is ubiquitous,
yet few can lay hands on one.
Inside its oval shell
it nurtures a serpent suckling
its own tail; both the departure
and the return, the danger
and the ultimate sanctuary.
When disturbed, zero is capable
of burning shadows in walls,
betraying the slick perfection
of its outer surfaces. When
nurtured, however, zero
can be induced to hatch
that resplendent swan
once observed by Rilke.

February: Sometimes Such Disparate Things

Sometimes such disparate things want to combine
to form a complex of sense, like a new thought
forming in a fecund world, its heretofore unacquainted
but suitably promiscuous elements discovering
the flesh of meaning where previously
there had been no matter, only the blank slate
of space. Sometimes it seems you could
take anything apart and with enough time
and patience arrange the pieces in a new way
that not only improves on the original, it alters
the entire system of awareness connected to it,
ushering in a grace of elevated
understanding that makes all prior problems
irrelevant. Sometimes it feels
like you have all the parts but only in the wrong
order, and then you realize that the order itself
is a part, apart, the missing part. If you could arrive
at the proper order (quest of the alchemists,
the emerald tablet), you would unlock the
structure and its meaning, and the meaning
would serve as a key to unlock all gates,
unbar all doors, remember all things forgotten,
erase all boundaries — ah, but there you arrive at chaos,
and you realize chaos is the key to order,
and the challenge is to apprehend chaos
while remaining sane, a soap bubble in the mouth,
leaving the disparate parts in their nebulous pattern
while sensing the implicit potential arrangements they carry:
their eyes distant, but with a certain body language
that suggests availability, interest, if only you
could utter the password to reach them.

The Old Flame Sublimated into Hermetic Metaphor

Say that I am a dark lake
nestled in the silence of a nighttime field,
off to the side of an Illinois interstate.
Occasionally the headlights of an approaching
car or truck on the highway find me,
and my surface flares into brief,
sudden life; wet electric star sparkle
that reveals my boundaries
but does not discover the old,
untouchable secrets I guard
in the depths of my silence, as the
headlights retreat and I vanish once more
into the uniform obscurity
of a Midwestern night in late November.

What I Mean to Say: June, 1984

When I say that the light of this memory
has an amber quality, what I mean is that we are insects
trapped inside it, trapped there still. We stood in the basement
of his grandparents' house, taking leave of each other
after a summer afternoon's adventures, not really wanting to.
He was a satyr in a sleeveless T-shirt and shorts,
just a few inches from me, so close to naked,
an eighteen-year-old god of the coming August. The stubble
on his jaw, the sweat in his sandy hair. We were so young.
And for once he didn't crack a joke, trigger some manic
diversion: It was as if the smart aleck had suddenly crashed
and left in its place something unreadable, a testing in his eyes,
as he reached out and gave my chin a soft, mock blow,
a substitute for something he couldn't say.

I stood paralyzed like a panicked animal.
We stood so close, we had been closer, but never so still.
I knew even then that I would regret my inaction,
that this moment was carving its initials in my heart.
And the moment went on long, surprisingly long,
but it did pass, pass while I froze. We said goodbye,
I went home shaking. The day became a coin,
a souvenir, a scar, a ghost in the system,
something to travel with me.

Now, seventeen years later, how I want to go back
and whisper in my own ear, "Take his dare."
How I want to tell myself what the moment was made of,
where to press, where to pause,
how to steer us both to the new territory
we wanted but couldn't find.

What I did at the time was reasonable:
The dangers were real, the unknown outweighed the known.
This is not a poem of regret: only memory, only desire.
Knowing what I knew then, I took the road to take.
But looking back, with the benefit of what came only later,
I can separate the good risks from the bad,
see the opportunities that would have yielded fortune,
like flashing lights on a map of the past.
I wish I could hand my past self that map like a pirate's scroll,
lead him to where the treasure of experience
lies still in the earth, waiting for his touch
to open the rusted clasp.

Tara

Tara of the kings, you are now
just a green hill in a country of green hills,
and no kings come to claim you;
only a half-dozen tourists in the morning,
who've been told you were once important,
who heard your name once in an American film.
But something in the soil remembers what you were,
remembers the stories, the moments you witnessed when
history passed from one hand to another,
when you were the pivot
around which the fate of kingdoms and armies turned.
No matter who comes and goes — and with or without
those people who stand on your windy height
to gaze for a moment into the greying distance
that surrounds you, and then head
back to the bus for lunch — they leave
and what you are stays behind, stays with you,
never passes with the minutes or the hours.
It's in the expression of the white horse who
guards the path that leads past the church
and through the cemetery to where you stand,
a thousand years and more, under grey skies
and blue, remembering your stories; stories
that surround you and never depart,
like the towering clouds
that always mass above you.

Night Diary for a Summer Afternoon

Asparagus flutters across the sun's ribs
and I am in my crystal kitchen,
taking the temperature of pineapples
and heads of state.
Your words come out
in spiderwebs,
jetting lazily across the
cool summer evening air
and a thousand
milkweed pods applaud.
The tubas
arrive with their
various regrettable casseroles;
I set the table with Fiestaware
and Dixie cups, pine cone centerpieces,
crazy straws. The monks enter
in their orange robes
and begin mingling with the tubas
and the absence of the Pyrenees,
who sent their regrets.
I wonder if things are going as well
as can be expected,
try not to notice the lengthening
shadows, the flash of fire
in the windows, the sudden
transparency
of my hand through which
patterns of waving grass
ripple and nod.

**Notes from first trip to San Francisco, 1986, 20 years old:
found scrawled in a spiral notebook fifteen years later**

Dec. 17, Wednesday.
First day: did Castro Street. Breakfast
at a place called "Welcome Home" (!)
Apple French toast, they're playing
Kate Bush and I think of D.
Shops: All American Boy, Rolo, Main Line.
Godzilla is really big here. They've got
the Gay flag. Everything is so funny;
people seem distant though.
I am strangely nervous.

I see a Humphrey Bogart movie:
As the organist (they have an organist)
is playing, an older woman next to me starts talking,
says the acting was better in those days.
Then she apologizes for talking over the organist.

Some of the men here are good-looking,
but too many moustaches,
and they never look at me.

I get a little lost, but find the
Walt Whitman bookstore: gay and lesbian books.
Joni Mitchell is playing. I buy $80 worth of books.
Also a metaphysical bookstore
called The Philosopher's Stone. I talk
to Ivan, who works there. Says he knows
Judy Grahn. I get the phone number of a
Wiccan group: Yule Solstice Ritual in a few days!
I buy another $80 worth of books.

I am in serious money trouble now,
and it's only my second day here.

Back in the Castro, I kill time
at the Patio Restaurant. I try cappuccino
and don't like it. It's all bitter!
The water has a lemon slice in it.

Lydia and I go to the Café Bohem.
I am too poor for anything
but bread & cheese.
Then we go to Polk Street.

Porn store: The Locker Room.
We go in, she for laughs, that's
my story too. Tension.
We meet this guy, clean-cut looking,
strangely sexy, who seems to be coming on
to both of us at once. He says:
"I'm not heterosexual, I'm not homosexual,
I'm just *sexual*."
Seems more interested in her than me.
She laughs at him, we leave.

I go to a meeting:
Gay and Lesbian Youth Group
up in the avenues. We talk for a while
on metal chairs, then go to a restaurant.
Everyone's nice, but it's only one evening,
too short to get to know anyone.

Gay newspapers: Campus Theater, "Live gay sex
on stage!" Massage, escorts.

On the streets,
no one makes eye contact.

Cliff House, Ocean Beach —
sign by the rocks:

CAUTION!
CLIFF AND SURF AREA
EXTREMELY DANGEROUS
People have been swept
from the rocks and drowned!

Upstairs
They bring me tea, Earl Grey,
a new discovery;
sun settles red into the Pacific.

Used book store, André Gide,
Fruits of the Earth:
"Melancholy is nothing but abated fervor."

Post script:
Two weeks later I fly back to Peoria,
still a virgin,
still wrapped too tight —
but I have danced the spiral dance in Berkeley,
met Laughing Sal in the beachside arcade;
and I know what pesto is now.

Awake While They Sleep

Awake while they sleep,
asleep while they wake;
brittle and soft
as the bread I break.

Bright lights after midnight,
moths on the moon;
and shadows that circle
from midnight to noon.

The buzz and the hum and
the booths full of boys —
ice water in glasses,
conversational noise.

And it's poems and french fries
and chocolate cake;
awake while they sleep,
asleep while they wake.

The sky is that eerie
electrical shade —
and we beat in the chest
of this city we've made,

And the nightflying insects
swarm neon and glass,
and they flicker and flutter
and swoop as we pass,

In the smooth asphalt silence
of the empty street,
and the deep summer night
made of darkness and heat.

Asleep while they wake,
awake while they sleep:
all good people outraged
at the hours we keep.

Chasing light with the creatures
who flutter and creep;
asleep while they wake,
awake while they sleep.

Churchyard in shadow,
floodlit lawn —
stone-covered Madonna,
waiting for dawn.

And the flock that surrounds her,
they twitch and they dance
in the pregnant air
and her unseeing glance.

Oh, the hours so short,
the shadows so tall,
but so deep they can hardly
be seen at all.

White Hen clerk,
sweet Latin smile —
shows me his bandage
and talks for a while

His teeth, his tattoo:
"See you later, man" —
lottery tickets,
shaving cream can.

And soiled in doorways
invisible men,
resting uneasy
like wolves in a den.

In the smooth asphalt silence
of the empty street,
and the deep summer night
made of darkness and heat.

After three, almost home,
only two more blocks:
resting my pad
on a newspaper box —

Scratch out some words,
make my peace with the night;
turn ink into sense,
and confusion to flight.

All alone with the creatures
who flutter and creep:
asleep while they wake,
awake while they sleep.

Avebury

She moved around the circle in the uncertain sunlight,
feeling those old stones one at a time.
The shadows of birds, clouds, houses,
armies passed by overhead to indicate the passing
of time. The stones felt coarse,
cragged, crabbed, full of friction and resistance,
worn smooth without polish, somehow,
yet rough as the hands of old men, older.
Their weight was beyond contemplation,
yet they seemed to rise up into the air,
floating like an exhibition of hot-air balloons,
dancing like a hallucination of elephants,
when she closed her eyes for a moment.
She wondered what they'd seen, wished they
could talk, understood that they could,
in fact, talk, wondered what they were saying,
telling her right now, things that she
would understand only later,
like when your computer downloads a file
while you sleep. She moved around the circle
slowly, the mud and the grass under her feet,
the breeze rippling her jacket, the sound of cars on
the highway bisecting her path. It took her most of the
afternoon to go round, bending over
each stone like a medic with a stethoscope.
There was a lot to listen to.
She wasn't in a hurry.
For thousands of years the stones had been
gathering words for the moment
when she asked them, "What have you seen?
What do you know?"

They had stood there observing,
listening, pondering, working out the answer to
the riddle they'd been given.
Their shadows swirled around them
in frantic circles, like the hands of clocks,
like "busy, working" symbols
on the faces of computer screens.
Some of the stones had
disappeared, carted away to make houses
in the village that sprang up nearby.
They had been chipped at for souvenirs, cursed
by sanctimonious infidels, shuddered at by
superstitious fools. Their
communion had been quartered by roadways,
disturbed by the rumble and fumes
of the automobile,
yet they stood and waited. Intact or not,
she knew they would
still be there, waiting, on the last day
the sun ascended above their horizon,
on the last day
when the sun looked down on their circle,
on their cold circle,
and asked them for their answer.

The Reader's Lament

The book offers sweet recess from the constriction
of being I; the footsore ego slips gratefully
into its warm bath of words, dissolves, floats,
is soothed and assuaged. The dreadful membrane
between earth and sky is weakened,
becomes permeable to spirits, messengers,
conduits of energy. The lonely receive guests
and the sick are liberated from their vessels.
The impossible becomes possible: Gravity is repealed,
suffering transformed into enlightenment,
nobility, meaning. Location becomes irrelevant.
For a time, time itself goes off the clock.

But soon, too soon, insistent alarms begin to sound
back in the world of dimension and gravity:
The covers must be closed, the body must resume its tasks,
the ego must re-coalesce, reapply its armor,
re-enter the fray. And oh, how the I howls
to remember itself, to leave behind the bath,
the bed, the sanctuary that allowed it, ever so briefly,
to untie the knots of separation and self-awareness
that bind it to itself.

First Entry: Sun., Feb. 03, 2002, 11:02 p.m. CST

At 10:57 p.m. on a cold Sunday night in early February, in a single precise instant I become aware of this thing which is blundering across a semi-deserted intersection in a residential neighborhood, watching the light about to go red. This thing is a specific and localized awareness caged in an animated cadaver, subject to time, gravity, and internal organic disturbances, dependent on a few rather limited senses for most of its information. Wherever I was before I got here, I am apparently stuck here now. Apparently this thing — *me* — has a name and a history and an identity, has been making all sorts of decisions, the consequences of which I am now subject to. I find that I can, with a slightly jarring effort, think back over this history, scanning the backstory that shapes and delimits my current situation no less restrictively than the body itself. This I that I now inhabit is undeniably and indelibly *on the record*. It has made enemies for itself, drawn far too much attention to itself on more than one occasion, squandered and mismanaged any number of resources and opportunities. There is little hope of fading quietly into the woodwork for a time to cogitate and chart a perfect course as if one had a clean slate. The program is in process, and my awareness has somehow blundered into it, completely ensnared. It's like being trapped inside a bad but preternaturally insistent video game. Worse, it appears that someone has been playing rather badly, in my name, for quite some time now. When will the quarter run out?

I become aware that the legs are walking, the feet swinging back and forth, carrying "me" along at a fair pace, without any conscious instruction to do so on my part. They just carry on with their business, step step stepping, as if we were all in perfect agreement here about where we were going and why. I am just a passenger along for the ride, up here in the head, like a child looking out the windows of an SUV on the Interstate wondering when he'll get where he's going. I know, by checking the records, that we are on our way back to "my" apartment. But it still seems odd to me that the feet are able to go about the business of taking me there without me actually telling them to. I realize that, at this point, I would actually have to issue a command to cause them to stop what they are doing. I would have to make a point of telling them, *Stop, feet, don't do the walking any more.* And then, because I am the boss of the feet, stop we would, still and sudden right here on this February sidewalk, hearing the sound of my visible breath, watching the shrubs behind the black wrought-iron fence of the apartment building I'm standing in front of stare back at me as if to ask what the hell I'm up to and why did everything suddenly stop?

I don't interfere with the feet. They are only doing what they believe is their business, and it's not like I've worked out any better plan of action than the going-back-to-the-apartment. Best to play along, for now. Try not to show weakness. Most of effective leadership is projecting the right air of confidence, right? The body has now stopped of its own accord (What, don't I even get to sign off on that? Do they have a stamp with my signature downstairs?) and the hands have produced keys from the pockets and are fumbling with them to unlock the door to the building. I scan the records again and discover that there are not expected to be any other humans waiting for me upstairs. Only a somewhat fractious and high-strung twelve-year-old black cat. Good, so I don't have to worry about being questioned too soon. Actually (continuing to scan), the cat is likely to subject me to a fairly intensive grilling, but the questions will all be in Cat so I should be able to more or less fake my responses, which the cat is pretty well used to anyway.

After exchanging a few diplomatic courtesies with the cat (who is actually involved in a tense negotiation with a shopping bag and so spares me little attention), the body heaves itself into a chair and the fingers begin frantically typing this account of my sudden shipwreck here on the shores of this exercise in three-dimensional constraint. They seem almost enthusiastic about it, though I'm not sure what business it is of theirs. Apparently the fingers are expressing some willingness to help me work this situation out, but I don't trust them. The records show that the body has a history of sabotaging our efforts in any number of ingeniously destructive ways. The body always knows exactly where to dynamite the tracks. It is capable of erupting with acne, warts, hernias, clogged sinuses, explosive flatulence, severe insomnia or several inches of extra bulk around the waistline — whichever will most effectively disrupt our plans or shatter our self-confidence — with impressively little notice. The body cannot be ignored, and a good relationship is to be striven for, but it certainly cannot be counted on as an ally going forward.

Meanwhile, the previous inhabitant of this life, if there was one, has not exactly left us a clean campsite. Just for starters, apparently something called "rent" is due within two days, there aren't enough resources to pay it, and there isn't enough lead time to generate them. The mind is expected to "think of something" before this deadline occurs. Moreover, notwithstanding our lack of rent-applicable resources, an unpleasant amount of fairly difficult work is supposed to be done this evening before rest is allowed, work which depends on the presence of inspiration not yet arrived. Once again, we are expected to "think of something."

We may or may not have the opportunity to update this report as the situation progresses. We are trying not to panic and do not want to cause undue worry about us. We would like to think that we will succeed in freeing ourselves from these circumstances in time — perhaps whatever metaphysical strands hold us here will suddenly fall away like fraying cobwebs if we simply struggle enough? — but for now we must play the hand we have been dealt. In the meantime, if any benevolent authority should read these words and become aware of our situation, we appeal to it for intercession, emancipation, justice.

To the Would-Be Shaman of the Urban Age

You can go, but you've got to come back.
If you make that journey through the membrane
that keeps us safe in the contents of our rational days,
if you go with presents and questions for those

immense gods who do not take your calls by day,
with messages for personages and ambassadors of dream —
give more than a passing thought to the return path.
Take string for the labyrinth, and preferably

an experienced guide. If you walk into the forest,
leave a trail of buttons, not breadcrumbs. And remember
that the membrane may be easier to penetrate than
it is to restore, and unless you know what

you're doing, you may return to the center
to find the center gone. You want to explore
those ghostly exotic cities on the ocean floor,
you want to pursue that numinous conversation

with the High Priestess just a bit further than
you've been allowed so far: You want to open the
roof of the cathedral to let in the whole vaulted sky.
These things are understandable, and it is not my

place to hold you back. But remember that once
there was extensive training for those who took
this path, a lore sadly lost to our time. Explore
if you must, but do not dive without a line:

Remember, you can go,
but you've got to come back.

Callanish in August

i

When he comes for us again
on the morning of solstice,
when everything heavy turns living and light,
we will be waiting for him, holding our breath,
still as a feather of stone.
The earth will carry us gently in its teeth
like a hatchling cradled in the mouth of a dog.
We will be bright as the dandelions,
gleaming like gneiss in the light of the lochs;
ready to be suspended between the winters again,
in that warm place between the columns of June and August.

ii

It's August, and glittering teeth of stone
rise up from the jaws of the earth. The king,
a blinding globe wreathed in gold, comes striding
down the double pathways of the stones in ceremonial
brilliance, full summer potency, a moment
intolerably bright; he turns to face his audience,
subjects and celebrants, flashes a last look of confidence
and then falls upon their swords. The shining
Scottish lakes on either side observe, as they always do,
in reflective silence. If they have anything to say
about the proceedings they keep it to themselves,
guarded in their depths. That first chill breeze
of autumn air comes from the sky; its blue deepens
and sharpens in a way that only happens here, like this.

iii

On a hill above a highway you find them,
crusty and reclusive, wild and curmudgeonly,
not tourist-friendly, not tamed by postcard racks.
They are like retired movie stars the world has forgotten,
withdrawn into their mansions, still living in
a different age with few doorways into our own.
They cluster in a circle
up here on their weedy height,
and think their rock thoughts, drawing the slow circles
of the sun in shadows on the grass,
and the occasional humans who blunder into their
presence are like gnats. The sound of the traffic
barely reaches them, is still somehow beneath
their notice. Their silence
dares you to try for their attention, to think of
something you could say that might engage them.
You want to earn their respect, the right
to stand among them, if only for a quarter
of an hour. They exist in a space
untroubled by time, and shrouded in a solitude
almost unimaginable
here in the city where I write. I conjure them now
on crowded buses, in supermarkets and cubicles,
anywhere, really,
when I need to impose on their grudging hospitality
again, when I need time
to go away for a while.

The Legend

Looking oddly serious in front of a red velvet curtain
you turned to look directly into the camera;
I remember the audience fell strangely silent
wondering what you would say.

    "Like children gathered around a campfire,
      my heart and I told each other stories to pass the time,"

ran the voiceover: so steady, so controlled
that I marveled at its composure —

    "to make the quivering stars seem less distant,
    the cool air less ponderous with darkness."

There was the sound of many pages turning
and a breeze that seemed to loft you along
through successive scenes of your life:

    "They were lies, all of them —
    beautiful stories of love and privation.
    They were like dark chocolate bon-bons
    nestled in the box."

There was that annoying comic routine of running
and not getting anywhere,
and a succession of guest comedians enabling inane pratfalls;
there was music, antique and warbling, radio static,
the distressed luster of time long gone;
and there was the sound of air leaking, your irreplaceable
reserves of hope gradually deflating,
barely audible under the laughter of the studio audience.

Judgment and Death of the Super-Villain

So finally, at five minutes past the end of time, after long and murderous pursuit up and down the aisles of the lifetimes and the centuries, you catch up with yourself, tackle and bind yourself, throw yourself down in chains and shackles. Now comes the cruel accounting: so many betrayals to avenge, such terrible questions to ask. Now, you think; at long last, *you will make that fucker pay*. There is no one to protect him, no one to stand in your way. All of the other characters have faded from the script. It's all played out, the milk spilled and the tears shed, and there is nothing left on the stage but you, yourself and the smoking pit into which you have cast yourself. There is no longer any authority to judge your blind, brutal vengeance: just the rag doll of yourself, your nemesis, to be beaten and broken for its treachery.

Of course, some satisfaction still eludes you. Even now, you refuse to answer your own direct questions; you will not cry out under your own hand. There is only mute animal suffering, not even a whimper of reproach. You will not meet your own eyes. And you continue to hold back the Great Secret, in some unreachable place. You will not explain, apologize, reveal anything of your own motivations to yourself: why you sold yourself to the Romans again and again; why you sang discord among the angel choir of your own creation; what you hoped to buy with the currency of your own defeat.

At the end of that torment, when the taste of your own blood is nothing to you, when you've exhausted your hate and your rage and there's no more strength in your arms to strike yourself, and you find yourself lying in the pit beside yourself, worn out, spent, naked, beyond memory or pain: There will be nothing left but to take yourself in your own arms and sleep together, your self and your dark self, wondering what it is that binds you beyond reason, at what point questions become their own answers, why the lover and the enemy come sewn together, inseparable. And only as these questions cease to make sense to you will you release yourself and your self into nothingness, the only shape where the two of you can exist in peace, as one: and only then will you understand that the Great Secret was not a dark corner of your soul but the main part of it, and the you that was separated from it the hapless aberration.

The DJ Considered as Mage
(for Dave and Kristine)

The celebrants arrive in the clearing for their revels,
an urban glade of brick and graffiti, ripped-up linoleum,
wax-stained carpet; the sacraments they receive are
liquid sound and light, scintillations and flashings in time
and space, the removal of certain barriers
and limits upon motion.

From behind a glass window above the magic circle,
like a sorcerer in his tower he takes spells from his grimoire,
spins them into lightning and wine. Mirrors and lasers
for his wizard's fire, gobos and strobes his arcane apparatus,
chemical smoke for the mists he must raise:
He makes it all leap whirling and sparking into
a system of interlocking hermetic gestures,
a divine clockwork of light, rhythm and melody,
the rapture of the dancers transmuting base metal
into a golden thread of ephemeral
but nonetheless transcendent evenings.

And the revelers are taken,
and the gates to the next world thrown open,
and the hours dissolve into ocean, Neptune's ballroom;
time a lattice of star-sparkle, a cup dipped
into the dark river of memory and oblivion.

We climb out through a small door in the skull,
leave it reluctantly open for the return hours later,
when the Mage must close his circle: when the storm dissolves
and the bric-a-brac whirled up to the heavens
is thrown back down gasping, sweating, exalted;
looking for diner food
and a bus ride home.

Reservoir

It's odd how she fills in the corners of your life, a liquid presence that merges with the darkness for a period of time and then detaches itself to brush against you, run between your legs when you walk; or you look up to find her watching you intently while you were concentrating on something else. There is this current of communication that never resolves itself into separate signals or symbols of meaning; it merely flows between two poles underneath the visible surfaces of the room, informing the space, giving the silence a thickened quality with another world lurking behind it, like a mirror in a Cocteau film. There is a charge that she pulls out of the atmosphere and relays to you, a deeper grid she connects to and graciously allows you to feed from her connection. And just as she studies you, and you find yourself reflected and captured in two yellow globes that suggest the moon at Autumn equinox, you know that there are times (or rather, there is a time) when she enters your mind and you remember something — not at any particular moment, but rather something that belongs to the undercurrent of untime that runs beneath and between the isolated moments like a water table. Just as she has her human moments of speech and meaning, when she sits up and asks you something so clear and unmistakable that she seems for a moment to be fully dressed, there are those times when you are blessed to inhabit the undivided space that is her element, sharing with her the ability to not just see things but rather see into, through and beyond them.

Immense Buddha Under Fire

For centuries your face stares out
from the face of an immense cliff,

unblinking, nearly changeless.
Stone lends you some of that detachment

you taught in life. You gaze out
over the plain, and what thoughts

are yours are not known even to you.
And these are the things you have:

Time that is nothing to you. Substance that you are
not aware that you have. Being that is neither

a verb nor a noun. And then one day they come
with guns and artillery, to untie the knot

that binds you into presence,
to shatter your meditation, your impassive

face sliding away into rubble and a smoke
of dust: the face you wore

before you were born. And after the collapse,
your outlines are precisely as solid

as they were before. These bits of rock
that come crashing down

might resemble tears, except that we know
you do not weep. It is only we who weep

at this destruction, and not necessarily for reasons
you would approve of.

The Writer's Prayer

I write these words knowing that no eye will ever read them and no ear will ever hear them. I write these words for no one but myself. These words will never be published, read aloud, disseminated, distributed, circulated or shown. These words are a secret between the ink that forms them and the paper on which they are written. I write these words from a place of utter security, knowing that what I say here need not impress or persuade, charm, amuse, uplift, comfort, move, or heal anyone anywhere, for no one but me will ever know they were written. They need rise to no standard of quality or art. These words serve no master but me, and convey no meaning but that which rests lightly on the surface of them, an ephemeral ripple moving vaguely across my consciousness. These words carry no responsibility and no agenda. They feel no pressure and honor no duty. These words will go into the wastes of time unregarded, unconsidered and unremembered. These words are free to be exactly and only what they are, what they were, what they will be; and then to evaporate, erasing themselves in their destined transcendence, returning to the original long word that contains all the other words, and from which they but briefly imagined themselves to be separated.

Post Script

There seems to be little left to say.
The cement mixers have left the stage;
the hyacinth, the apostrophes, the milk duds
all used up. Gone and gone.
The conductor is still beating out time of course,
as a matter of form, in a formal
and obligatory way. And frame after static,
empty frame still flickers on the screen.
But you and I know the score,
know the birds fled south long ago,
know the last ship sailed for the west
and the dance floor is empty.
Those old sets have been torn
down already: the house where we
grew up, and the more ramshackle one
where we almost kissed, but didn't,
that nerve-soaked night in college.
So why do we stick around?
Why does the air hush and freeze
around us as if there were one thing left
unfinished, when we know that
the story's pockets are
empty, the charge spent?
Is it possible that the tale
only really begins after the last
page has been turned, the book
closed and put aside,
the reading lamp switched off?

Dooncarton
(for Corbin and Tracy)

What's left of a place
when you subtract the place itself is the people
who were there at the same time, or maybe the complex
of associations that were formed there, or something
true that seemed to emerge from the place and became
a souvenir: something discovered that remains
with one even when the place has been left behind,
grants one the power of return at will,
a center that moves with consciousness.

In this case picture three small figures stumbling
exhausted out of a rental car at dusk,
three figures who are such a tiny part of
this immense, intricate landscape, this complicated
enormousness of hills painted with light and water,
that the human field of vision seems a poor,
constrained thing, able to take in so little of
such color and distance.

In a patch of green grace
on a subtle but well-placed rise,
we discover the objects of our pilgrimage:
a humble yet enigmatic circle of seven stones,
too small to attract the masses, no plaques or gift shop,
just 4,000 years of presence. Small but dignified rocks
hugging their secret pasts, their millennia of silent watch,
looking out across the water to hazy Rinroe point;
the difficult questions now resolved, forgotten or laid aside,
only time on its long journey, time and silence.

Wondering what sort of people came here then,
under this sky, reflected over this water,
with what hopes and deaths and blessings
did they charge this ground, these stones as witness?
See this place as a country chapel
for a different kind of churchgoer, place where
the earth met sky, where the circle gave strength.

And us on our own night, standing with eyes closed,
each to each her own moment, his own vision:
for me, a long-absent voice
quoting wise words from across the water;
Beloved, gaze in thine own heart...

We took that circle inside and took it with us,
left it behind us, never moved from the spot:
having driven so far, through wild Connemara
and water-colored Mayo,
having braved barbed wire and sheep shit
for this triangle of hands and silence,
a prayer in the twilit Irish air,
a place that will endure when
the place itself is behind it.

Immensity

Your immensity is something you keep
under lock and key because it is terrifying to you.
At night your immensity wakes you up,

banging its metal cup against the bars
of the cage where you keep it. Your immensity
wears seven-light-year boots and can cross

between stars with a single stride. Your immensity
can look at a table or a refrigerator or a window
and see each separate particle that makes it up.

Your immensity's head is the size of the rolling earth,
and its dreams boil like magma inside a skull of rock.
From time to time an island in the Pacific erupts

and you know a terrifying clarity, terrifying because
it does not last, cannot help you in the everyday
routine where you exist without your immensity,

because you don't know what to do with it,
how to take it out in public, how to teach it
to work with you in the world

rather than turning you into a fool with glazed,
vacant eyes. So you make your immensity wait
until you're ready for it, until you're done

with the world, until you're ready
to leave behind the beloved things
that your immensity dwarfs.

Big Glass Jar

Monologues & Stories
1990-1999

Directions to the Directions:

In order to present these pieces as uncluttered texts for reading, stage directions have not been included in the text itself. Instead, where applicable, stagings are described in the "Notes" section at the back of the book.

The Idea of You

I called you up and I asked how were you and could I please speak to the Idea of You?

You said, "Excuse me?"

I said I didn't call to talk to you, I called to talk to the Idea of You. I said I had been doing some thinking. I had realized that all the time I had been seeing you, it was really the *idea* of you I wanted to go out with. You asked me how I had come to this astonishing conclusion. I said, Oh, little things tipped me off: the way you knocked over your water glass last Wednesday, when the idea of you was grace and ease. The way you fumbled for words on Sunday, but the idea of you always knew what to say. I said I always understood the idea of you, but lately you were beginning to confuse me.

There was a momentary pause as you handed over the receiver, and then a voice came on the line that reminded me of you but without those annoying glitches and halts. We talked for a few minutes in what felt like a carefree, ideal way; and then the Idea of You asked to speak to the Idea of Me. I asked for clarification of this bizarre suggestion — and it asserted that the Idea of Me was too sensitive and intelligent to reject the human imperfections of someone I loved.

Sensing that I had somehow dropped the ball, I nobly stepped aside — so that the Idea of Us could live happily ever after.

Young Person's Guide to Synchronicity

There was this man who lived in a house and this man who lived in a house lived with some cats and the thing about this man who lived with these cats was he didn't live with one cat two cats or even four or five cats, he lived in a house with 365 cats. And the thing about these cats was that instead of being named ordinary cat things like for instance Daisy or Tiger or Feedbag, they each were named with a date, like for instance October the 3rd, or March 28th. And if you went over to his house you'd be sitting in a chair talking to him and a cat would jump in your lap, start to paw you and claw you like cats do when they think you're someplace good to sleep and you'd say, Hey, what's the name of this cat? And the man, the man would think for a minute and then he'd tell you a date, like for instance May 12th — and you'd look kind of freaked out because May 12th just happened to be your birthday. Only, it wasn't always your birthday, sometimes he'd say September 26th and you'd have to think for a minute to remember that was your parents' wedding anniversary, or August 4th which was the day Vance Williams fell off of Mrs. Paluska's sailboat and died because his heart stopped. Only sometimes you couldn't remember that date at all so the man, the man would look at you and go and get a book off the shelf and say:

"June 17th. Day you fell down in the swimming pool age four and developed your fear of the water. Reason you don't drink."

"January 9th. Day you figured out how to masturbate."

"November 26th. Day you realized that you weren't the only one who had an unhappy childhood."

And then the man would look at you like you were a diagram explaining how to fix a broken radio, sit back down, ask you what you planned to do with your life. And you, you'd look back down at that cat like how could it possibly know what it knew, and its eyes would be blank...like two empty marbles.

A Poverty of Murk

I loved you and you asked me to tell you all my secrets and because I loved you I told them to you and then you didn't love me and I didn't love you and I had the feeling that I didn't have any secrets anymore, so I went looking for some.

I felt strangely empty, like a pocket turned inside out, nothing inside but a few loose threads and some bits of lint. I would look at other people's secrets and consider whether I wanted to adopt them as my own, but none of them really embarrassed or discomfited me the way a good secret should. I tried inventing a few secrets but none of them had real guts or teeth.

At this point it occurred to me that my lack of secrets was in itself a kind of secret and that this secret was perhaps the most shameful and disturbing secret of all. And so I began to behave as if I had many secrets, strange and reprehensible and possibly illegal ones, to draw arbitrary, invisible boundaries in conversation that others must not step across without encountering a sudden chill or a silent rebuke.

And so I concealed myself behind deep layers of intrigue and deceit so that no one might glimpse the fact that I was a hollow person without scandal or skeleton. And I found that I was happy then, because I felt young again, and romantic, and capable of being betrayed.

The Day of Your Return
(for René Magritte)

This is the time you turn the TV set on and nobody's there,
nobody but a ghost in a pink striped suit playing
"Don't Leave Me This Way" on a slide trombone.
This is the time your breath packs its suitcase
and heads for the Alps with your spirit in tow,
singing the song about the rocking pony,
about the circus that hangs in the air above the sea.
This is the day the clock whispers everything it knows
to the chair and the dining room table.

This is the day that the telephone rings
and when you pick it up it says, "Hello. I am your phone.
What did you have for lunch today?"
This is the day that dairy products shaped like fish
swim by outside your dining room window.
This is the day before the day after the day
you learn how to speak in the language of dishes and umbrellas,
the day you realize that home is a little door
in the side of your head,
and the porch light is always on.

This is the day that you step outside your door but a hand
has yanked the ground away and you drift, through a
powder-puff painting of pink and orange light, to a land where
lips live in peace without heads, and everyone
drinks sugar from glasses shaped like harmonicas.
This is the day you look into the sink and finally notice
the tiny family living there.
This is the day you finally get some mail.

Story #423

A friend of mine got on the el train the other day and a man was sitting there holding a large balloon in his lap. The man himself was paying no attention to the balloon, but everyone around him was staring at it intensely. It was like they were fascinated by it, like they couldn't take their eyes off of it. Finally the man spoke. He said: "You can all go fuck yourselves. Quit looking at my fucking balloon." The people looked at the floor. The train stopped and the man got off.

Two stops later a woman got on carrying a tank with a small lizard. Everybody very conspicuously avoided looking at the lizard. After a few minutes of this the woman lifts up the cover of the tank and the lizard says, "Jeez, relax, wouldja? It's not like I'm a goddamn *balloon*."

Between The Lines In 4/4 Time

I don't remember what the song was but I remember us dancing in the basement of his house. It was New Year's Eve, I was sleeping over...we weren't sleepy.

We'd been learning dance steps in PE that semester: foxtrot, waltz, tango. A slow song we liked was playing on the stereo and he said, very casually:

"Hey — let's practice our dance steps."

I remember that we had to figure out who would lead and who would follow. I think we took turns. I remember how wonderfully strange his hand felt in mine. Not like a girl's at all. And yes, when our bodies were pressed together I could tell that he wasn't just thinking about the dance steps. He had pale blue eyes, just like the Lou Reed song.

That was the only time we danced together. If the truth be told, it was the only time we ever really touched each other, except for a hand on the shoulder. We both took girls to the senior prom.

Every now and then one of my straight friends asks me:

"Tell me, Dave, what was it like growing up gay? That must have been hard. High school, I mean. Dating."

And I tell them that it was just like growing up straight, except that you had to learn how to fill in the blanks and appreciate the almosts; that sometimes the things that didn't happen were more important than the things that did.

Jimmy, Roger & John

Seven years ago when you came to the city as a green gay kid with wide eyes and empty pockets, you saw the golden boys dancing in the clubs, sweaty and ecstatic, like faerie kings at the height of their glamour with smooth muscles, puppy dog eyes and promising artistic careers.

You saw their names on posters on lampposts, you saw their paintings in cafés and their drawings on T-shirts in stores and they left you five dollar tips on five dollar checks when they had coffee at the restaurant where you worked.

Five years later you saw some of them walking with canes: observed from bus windows making slow deliberate steps across crosswalks on cold winter afternoons, or sitting in cafés with friends to help them stand and sit, like old men at 28, seeming alternately courageous and confused.

Some of the people you know who are dying young are artists. Some of them are artists like Shelley and Rimbaud, who produced their greatest work before their mid-twenties. They will be remembered. Some of the people you know who are dying young are artists like Walt Whitman or René Rilke, who produced their greatest work in their later years. They will not be remembered because their train got derailed before it pulled into the station.

And then one night in a darkened movie house you see a trailer for a movie in which Dustin Hoffman chases a diseased monkey around wearing a yellow plastic suit, and you are mildly startled to remember that there are still people in the world for whom the idea of a plague is still a good subject for entertainment. You wonder if *Longtime Companion* would have done better at the box office if only it had had a few more children and animals in it.

You go home alone. You call one of your friends who's still alive and you don't talk about the past. You talk about the future.

Told Me What?

I've always hated him; sometimes I think he's the only person I ever really did hate. I hated him when he threw rocks at my sister and left her with a bloody face; I hated him in eighth grade when he calmly picked me up off the mat and broke my leg in two. And before I ever knew I was gay, he did: He'd sneak up next to me in the locker room, grab my hand, yell out to the guys, "Hey look, Davey's my *boyfriend*," and he always got his laugh. Oh, yes, not only was he bigger and stronger and meaner, but the *people* loved him. His jokes always laid the room flat, and besides, in a world of morons a bludgeon passes fine for a rapier.

Time came though, when it seemed he was losing ground. People growing up, getting smarter, shedding by degrees the cruelty of children, and here's where I give him credit for foresight — he saw the writing on the box top, knew he was past his date and he was losing the room, so he went away, cleaned up his look, got himself a brand-new act.

And one day when I'd almost forgotten him, there he was on TV, shark-smug and vulgar as ever, and the jokes weren't any better, the same broad smack of the bully's board, but the *strategy* — sweet Mary, the slippery nerve! What made me sit up and whistle is the way he'd switched all the name tags in the middle of the night. By the time I'd tuned in, he had half the room going that he was the victim, that everyone he'd ever bullied had really given him the Dutch rub for the last nine rounds. Oh, I had to love it even while I remembered how to hate him; the *stories* he told, see, it was me out of line in the locker room, flogging the piss out of him with my lavender limp wrists, and my sister on the play-ground shoving bloody rags in his face, and wasn't it hard to be a great big vulnerable guy like him but he'd pay us all back now with jokes he got from a God who loved the underdog. And I listened to the people loving him again, for giving them back their childhood of blunt and heavy and hard, and the most delicious of chocolate-dipped, honey-covered lies: that they could have the spoils of the victor *and* the righteousness of the oppressed; welcoming me to a brand-new world in which every Goliath can paint himself as a David.

Freedom
(for Chuang-tze)

It was a week before the inauguration and Bill Clinton was walking down the bank of a river or creek to set a frog free. The frog belonged to Chelsea, who had requested that it be set free so that it could be allowed to live a quote normal life unquote. I was watching a chubby 46-year-old-man scramble down a hillside, followed by easily twenty or thirty men and women with microphones, cameras, tape recorders and note pads, there to document the most powerful man in the western world bestowing the gift of freedom on a mostly oblivious frog. I tried to imagine where this frog would be in say, four years, enjoying what so many Haitians had so recently been denied; whether it might pause from time to time to pinch itself in froggy gratitude, if only it had fingers to do the pinching. I wondered also exactly how many people in the world are living lives that could be described as quote normal unquote; and if it's true, as I suspect, that the vast majority of people live their lives in cages, either visible or invisible, chosen or thrust upon them — then the freedom to spend one's life half-submerged in mud, owing allegiance to no creature and no state, should perhaps not be described as "normal," but the gift of a century, or a lifetime; and then I thought I understood why those reporters were there.

Painting for an Empty Canvas

In a perfect world, there would be a painting on the screen right now — in a world where performance artists always had access to the perfect visual aid on very short notice. I can't tell you what the painting itself would look like. Perhaps I would be asking you to admire its bold use of color, or the touching expression in the eyes of one of its figures, or just a certain awkward sincerity. Maybe there wouldn't be much of anything to admire about the painting itself, but by looking at it you'd understand that it was painted by a human being who had some talent or no talent or a lot of talent, however the universe might decree. A human being who was killed on June 26 by a Tomahawk missile that missed its target in Iraq.

Her name was Leila Al-Attar, and she was one of Iraq's leading painters, and she and her husband were found dead in the rubble of their house after the attack. At this point I would mention that six other civilian people were killed in the bombing and a dozen more maimed, and the fact that they hadn't painted anything didn't make their lives and families and concerns any less important. I would then explain that this attack was launched by a man who knew very well that some of the missiles would probably miss their targets and go into civilian areas, and that while I voted for this man and spent a year working to elect him, and out of political necessity I will vote for him again, my... admiration for him has been dealt a possibly fatal blow. In a perfect world there would be a painting on the screen right now. But there isn't a painting, and it doesn't really matter because there isn't a painter anymore either.

Parts of Me Function Like a Dream

I think I first noticed something weird was going on about the time I learned how to read. There was this fast-food restaurant by our house and every day we drove past it on our way to other places. Well, they had one of those magnetic signs with letters you can rearrange to spell out different messages and one day we were driving by and the sign said:

TRY OUR ROAST BEE

Now, as a child I was upset and disturbed by bees in any context, but eating them seemed out of the question. When I asked my parents about it, they told me that I was just confused, that the sign must have said, "Try our Roast *Beef*." But I knew what I'd seen and I continued to watch the sign warily for two months, until it changed again to read:

TRY OUR CHICKEN SAND

If anything, I found this idea more disturbing than the Roast Bee. But I knew by this time that no one would believe me, so I kept it to myself. After that the course of my childhood was more or less set. Things that made no sense seemed to follow me around like packs of dogs that smelled an easy meal. I met lunatics on the bus who could read my mind, I had one friend who could answer the telephone with his feet, and for five years the number 36 stalked me everywhere I went. Gradually I realized that the world was intrinsically strange, and I don't just mean strange around the edges, I mean strange at its core.

So by the age of 11, when I began to figure out that men were more beautiful to me than women — that boxer shorts were more intriguing to me than, say, negligees — well, I knew because of the Roast Bee and the Chicken Sand that the world and I were going to spend a lot of time disagreeing about what was strange and what wasn't, what was truth and what was confusion.

PARTS. PARTS. FUNCTION.
DREAM. LIKE. A.

As a child I saw faces everywhere I looked; the world seemed overpopulated with faces. House with two windows for eyes and a driveway smile; silhouettes in wood-grain walls; cars with headlights for eyes and a bucktooth license plate.

As an adolescent, I spent a lot of time wondering whether I was dreaming the world or the world was dreaming me. And I thought that if the world was dreaming me, well, that might explain the expressions on all those faces.

If, on the other hand, I was dreaming the world, it would explain those moments when the world seemed like just an extension of myself — I had cameras for eyes, radios for ears, all the books in the library for my memory; other people's lives and personalities seemed like subsets of my own life, and stories in novels seemed like fragments of my story. I realized that "I" was made up of countless strange parts that acted independently of each other but somehow connected back to the center.

And that sensation, in turn, explained a particular kind of shock I would feel upon realizing, suddenly, at the oddest of moments, that I was a particular person, with a particular face and a particular identity. For a long moment I would feel very uncomfortable about this, as if I'd been cast in some randomly-chosen part when all I really wanted to do was watch the play. But there I was, wearing the costume, speaking the lines, and what bothered me most was a nagging feeling that if I chose to let it, the whole thing could continue to run all by itself, without the slightest effort on my part. I think I've spent the last dozen years trying to figure out how to take charge of the production.

PARTS. PARTS. FUNCTION.
DREAM. LIKE. A.

City Dream #8

And so time spiralled and twisted in its marble track and the people built cities, great cities so tall and wide and elaborate that eventually the people lost all memory, one by one, of all of the ways out of the cities.

And the people lived in the cities and the people lived in the cities and a great age came and went. And time twisted again in its marble track and eventually, as the years and decades passed, the old religions began to die, winking out one by one like Christmas lights on a faulty line, and the people grew restless and dull and desperate, and more years went by, empty and godless, until finally the people began to search for new gods to console them and occupy their adoration.

And like their most primitive ancestors, the people naturally began to look for gods in the world around them. But the world had changed and changed again, and so in place of the trees and the rivers and the rocks the people began to worship the great presences of the city: the Sky Scrapers, great mountains of steel and glass; the Bridges, mysterious structures connecting distances across unpassable chasms; the Traffic Lights, strange guardians of crossroads and highways.

They burned incense at the feet of lightposts and mailboxes; el stations became chapels of prayer where pilgrims would gather, chanting and praying and dancing the dervish on wooden platforms, and when the low rumble of a train approached and built to a passionate shaking the faithful would rend their garments and begin speaking in tongues of prophecy and blessing.

And what with all the chanting and the praying the tremendous din of it all finally reached the ears of the old gods in their mountains and rivers and caves, and being gods they were unable to resist the smell of all that incense and adoration and so they came, the old gods came: They left their rivers and rocks and trees and took up residence in the el trains and the office buildings, they checked into mailboxes and traffic lights, and those old gods became new gods then, and they grew in power with each new believer until they became mighty and numerous as in times of old, able to perform miracles or let loose plagues, capable of shaking the earth with a thought or blotting out the sun with an angry gesture.

And gradually the gods of the city learned the duties and offices that came with their new shapes: how to grant small miracles to the virtuous, like unexpected parking spaces or on-time trains, as well as curses for the impious, like elevators too packed to get on, or buses splashing mud on a brand new suit. And time twisted again in its marble track, as we lived out our days in the blessings of steel and glass, the beatitudes of the Holy City.

Please Drive Slowly

Please drive.
Please drive slowly.
Please drive slowly when driving in this neighborhood.
Please drive. Please drive slowly.

Please drive slowly because children.
Please drive slowly because children may be playing
in this neighborhood.
Please drive. Please drive slowly.
Please drive slowly because children
may be playing in this neighborhood
who have no hands and no feet.
Please drive.
Please.
Please drive slowly.

Please drive slowly because children may be playing in this
neighborhood who have no hands and no feet and who are rolling
small objects which are *indistinguishable* from their own heads.
Please drive.
Please drive slowly.

PLEASE DRIVE SLOWLY BECAUSE SMALL CHILDREN
WITH CHOPPED OFF HANDS AND CHOPPED OFF FEET
MAY BE GLEEFULLY KICKING THE DECAPITATED
HEADS OF OTHER CHILDREN IN FRONT OF THEM IN
THE GUTTER.

...Please drive.
Please drive slowly.

An American Childhood

As a small child I lived in a lighthouse. My whole family lived in the lighthouse, which worked out pretty well as we were all tall, skinny people. At night, I would glance up from my homework and pause to look out the single window at the ships passing slowly back and forth on the horizon, wondering if any of them would encounter the homemade explosive mines my older brother and I had set up in the harbor. Most nights I was still gazing out the window when my sister entered the room, with her enormous leathery wings and the long purple tongue that unrolled like a party favor from her mouth. As we spoke, the tongue would carefully probe and explore every tiny little crack and cranny of the room, searching for small insects and fingernail clippings to provide her with protein to help nourish the huge, organic experimental space station that was growing from the back of her head. It was fun growing up in a lighthouse. I hope to return there someday, with presents for all of my family, but I have promised myself that first I must save enough money to have my head surgically reattached to my body so that I do not frighten them on my return, especially my sister, who is very sensitive after all.

Justice Takes a Road Trip Part II

Somewhere on death row a black man is waiting to be executed for a crime he didn't commit because he doesn't exist. Somewhere on death row a black man who doesn't exist is waiting to be executed for the crime of murdering two small boys by drowning. The black man who doesn't exist was created by a white woman who does exist, and who did indeed murder two small boys by drowning, but who will not be executed because the jury felt that she'd had a troubled life and didn't get the help she needed. The black man who doesn't exist also had a troubled life and didn't get the help he needed.

In fact, there are large numbers of black men on death row now, all of whom exist, and all of whom had troubled lives and didn't get the help they needed. When the black man who doesn't exist is executed, they will ask him for his last words and this is what he will say: "A hammer without a handle is not a good hammer. A car without a steering wheel is not a good car. And a law which cannot be applied fairly is not a good law. Read the statistics. How many black people who are convicted of murder get the death penalty? How many white people who are convicted of murder get the death penalty? Read the statistics."

And then he dies.

Stonewalled, or The Sound of the Crowd

I've always found something faintly horrifying about the sound of a large crowd cheering. It's one of the reasons I don't like sporting events, one of the reasons why those pep assemblies back in high school used to make my blood run cold. Even concerts do it to me sometimes, even when I love the band and want to cheer myself. Maybe it's because of all the atrocities that people around the world still gather in large groups to cheer — torture of humans and animals, floggings, bullfights, executions.

I think of the crowd that packed into a stadium in Afghanistan recently to watch three men be buried alive for committing what the law calls "sodomy." According to an Amnesty International report, the men were placed in front of a wall of stone, and while thousands of people watched, a tank drove into the wall and toppled it onto them. The men lay pinned under the rubble for half an hour. Two of them died the next day, the third is...believed to have survived. A month later two boys were bulldozed under a wall of dried mud. They were 18 and 22 years old, respectively.

I wonder at what age they began to feel sexual attraction to men. I wonder how long they struggled with their feelings before they finally reached out to touch another man, whether they understood as they reached out that the touch would mean lying mangled and suffocating under several tons of mud. Whether they heard, from somewhere, the sinister sound of cheering carried faintly on the wind.

I wonder what they think about as they wait to die. I imagine that on a warm spring night like tonight, as countless cocktails are being raised in the bars along Halsted Street, as men are touching freely in the dark corners of Man's Country or the Unicorn, and I sit here on stage as an open — or, as they used to say when I was growing up, "avowed" — homosexual, at the very same moment an 18 year-old boy is sitting in a cell or dungeon somewhere, knowing that within 24 hours he'll learn what it's like to have a wall of rocks collapse on him. And, if he survives the initial impact, to lie pinned underneath it, crushed and bleeding. While no one comes to help him. While thousands cheer.

The Age of Disease Part I

We were talking, he and I. We were talking about the future, or rather I was, or rather, I was trying to. He kept changing the subject. Finally he said, "The future? What's that? You talk about the future if you want to. I don't even know what it is anymore." He told me it was time for him to take some pills. He left for a few moments, then he came back.

"The future," he said. "Let me tell you about the future. There was a night a couple of weeks ago, with really bad fog. I mean just awful. I was out on the interstate driving, and the fog was so bad I couldn't see more than three feet in front of my bumper. After that there was nothing. I couldn't think about getting home, I couldn't think about the next exit ramp. All I could think about was right now, was the road under my tires. And whether or not the fog was getting worse. And that" — he said — "that's what it's like being alive now. In the late 1990s. End of the century. The Age of Disease. HIV. Hepatitis C. Cancer. Lymphoma. Leukemia. Tuberculosis. Gulf War Syndrome. Ebola. *E. coli.* Mad Cow Disease, for Christ's sake. No one I know can see more than five years ahead of them and if they tell you they can they're either lying or clueless. As far as I'm concerned," he said, "the future has disappeared. The future is a tangle of dead ends, washed-out bridges, invisible ice patches. And the distance between the edge of the fog and my bumper gets a little smaller every minute."

Davy Jones in the Produce Department:
A Piscean Parable

He went to the supermarket to buy some melons he had a thing for melons lately you could say he was on a melon "kick" and it was there in the produce aisle of the Jewel that he saw her a sort of elven princess with long green hair and a crown of bones she was examining some kiwi he wanted to ask her a question but he wasn't sure what it was it was on the tip of his tongue but every time he tried to get a fix on it it went away somewhere she was examining a bag of spinach but in her hands it looked like kelp nobody else seemed to notice her crown of bones or if they did they must have figured she was on her way to a costume party but he knew better she was an elven princess consort of the Sea King daughter of Leviathan sister to Triton hence the hair like seaweed and a headpiece clearly fashioned from the bones of drowned men and women he wanted to ask her a question but every time he tried to look at her he became confused and turned back to the melons perhaps it was just as well he thought you know how the fairy folk play games with time I could wake up in the bread aisle fondling a bag of hot dog buns in the year 2284 then a voice spoke in his ear he was afraid to turn around it said *I couldn't help noticing you staring at me* he said I was trying to stare but I kept getting confused she said *I'm here because you're drowning* he said I'm only here to buy some cantaloupe she said *If you touch them they'll turn to boulders that drag you down into the pitchdark crevices of the sea* he said thanks for the bulletin what about some honeydew she said *You have more time than you think but less than you want* he said is that a wig it looks like a wig and the bones look plastic she said *I have the ability to rescue you but I need you to concentrate* he said if I could concentrate I suppose I wouldn't be drowning and she replied with *a complex mathematical formula* and then he was falling into the pitchdark crevices and he heard her saying *If you take a very deep breath* he heard her saying *a very deep breath* she told him to take *a very deep breath* and *it just might last you* she said *it just might last you until you see your way out* and he took a breath and most of the breath was water and the water was everywhere and the question then was how much did he care and how long could he survive on the memory of air and how badly did he even want to come out on the other side?

X-Punch 2K

It's a lazy Saturday afternoon, the kind I haven't had in years, and I'm having one of those *Peanuts*-style philosophical conversations while hanging out behind a low generic brick wall with Ernie, Cookie Monster, and a Boxing Alien with Glow in the Dark Eyes. Ernie says, "Gosh, Sesame Street sure has changed since the aliens started moving in." Cookie Monster doesn't say anything, he just crunches up a cookie in his mouth without actually eating it. You know, like he does. Ernie says, "You know, I mean these new *scary* aliens, not the furry kind that just said 'Yep' and 'Nope' all the time. They were always very friendly." The Alien doesn't say anything, he just starts punching me. I ignore him. Ernie says, "I read an article on the Internet about a restaurant that got bombed the other day. A man who was there when the bomb went off said that one minute he was eating his dinner, the next minute he was surrounded by people who were missing arms and legs. He said there was blood everywhere." Cookie Monster says, "Me no like to read articles on the Internet. Me long for a simpler time when there was no Internet, no e-mail, no pagers, no cell phones. How me supposed to eat cookies in peace? Me wish there were no aliens either. Ever since me started watching *The X-Files* me have nightmares all the time." The Alien begins punching Cookie Monster. Ernie says, "I can't help wondering how long it will be before the bombs are made with plutonium instead of fertilizer." Cookie Monster, nearly dead from The Alien's repeated blows, gasps out his last words, "Me no understand why we can't all just get along," and then dies. Ernie says, "Have you noticed how the aliens are always malevolent bloodthirsty sleestaks now? When I was young the aliens were always benevolent. They wanted to help people. I used to imagine climbing on board their spaceship and going with them and it was always nicer where they came from. They had everything all worked out." We don't say anything else for a long time. I keep waiting for the last panel because I know it will wrap everything up with a nice neat punch line, but the last panel doesn't seem inclined to help us out so we sit; tensely, nervously, uncertain what's expected of us.

The Language Families

I saw a woman on the train. She was reading a book, like many of the people on the train, and I could see the title on the spine of the book. The book was called *Language Families*. The train kept rattling on, charging through the underground tunnel, lights rushing past the windows like the flickering of a strobe. I started to wonder about the Language Families. About the Language Families and what they must be like.

The Language Families live in elaborately structured homes in which each room is predicated on the one before it. The children are not raised on milk from their mother's breasts; rather, she bends over them and whispers a cool stream of words into their open mouths: protein-rich nouns, carbohydrate-laden verbs, chewy, fibrous prepositions and later, once they're teething, lots of crunchy adjectives to cut their teeth on. The children, like their parents, grow up hungry for long, rich, exotic sentences, which are subsequently broken down into etymological fragments of meaning in the ruminations of their four-chambered stomachs. The Language Families do not spend their quality time on picnics by the beach and campfire cookouts; rather, oratory and declamation are their games of choice.

The Language Families do not sire sons and daughters, but prosaists and poets. The prosaists pay the bills, bake the bread, mow the lawns, and wash the dishes; while the poets light candles, utter prayers, water the gardens, care for the aged, and bandage the wounds of the children, who bleed dreams, fairy tales, and journal entries. And at night, when the children are safely in bed, mumbling fragments of nonsense as they descend the staircases of sleep, down toward the Indo-European foundations of speech, their parents crawl into beds of subtext and connotation, where the poets make seething, passionate love to the prosaists — who can never, never get to sleep.

Points of Connection

I have never been one to travel in straight lines if I can avoid it, nor do I speak in direct sentences usually, feeling that the shortest distance between two ideas is usually a meandering Sunday stroll.

But though the mind travels in circles and spirals and knots, the body moves faithfully in a straight line through time, slowly, relentlessly, from moment A to moment B, from year X to year Y, with enough surety and determination that you begin to know, in the very caverns of your soul, that there is no Z your mind can posit in time that your body will not sooner or later arrive at.

For instance Patrick, dead in his coffin. His face looking waxed and artificially colored under the saccharine funeral home lights, looking more like a made-up mannequin than the needy, vehement Irishman who taught me astrology and patience at a mostly empty café on Sunday afternoons. Patrick arrived at his point Z. Quite suddenly, without warning really: a bicycle in the blind spot of a truck and a phone call after midnight and there I am on a senselessly hot August afternoon, looking at the mannequin they made out of my friend.

Patrick had, perhaps, a lifetime to contemplate point Z as his mind made loops and crosses trying to avoid it or understand it, defeat it or transcend it, but when he reached his point Z without warning his body moved straight through time into its embrace, regardless of the mind's need to vector or circumnavigate. Patrick's point Z came before my point Z so I was able to regard it from the vantage point of say, M or N. By the time I'd made it to P or Q I'd learned that the awareness of Z didn't bring it any closer or push it farther away, could neither slow nor speed its progress.

But I don't mean to equate point Z solely with death. There are Z's and there are sub-Z's, and alphabets within alphabets as the body moves through time. Consider point A the moment you wake alone in bed in a patch of sunlight and realize that it's been a long time since a man really touched you. I mean really touched you in a way that makes you stretch like a cat every time you think about it in the weeks and months to come. Now consider point D the moment, perhaps hours later or perhaps weeks or months, when you lock eyes with a man who seems to know you the way bees know clover. Consider point M the connection, the point of intersection for the lines described by your body and his as they move through time.

And point Z? It's not the point that comes immediately after you've gone your separate ways, or even three or four points later when you've gained a little distance on it and can think about it clearly. No, point Z is a place in time, maybe moments away or years, when point M no longer seems quite real, is so far away that it almost seems irrelevant.

I have spent years in love with a certain man, and seen point M, when it arrived, seem flimsy and meaningless. An idle conversation in his basement at 2 a.m. when it became clear the TV interested him more than I did, or that time we danced and I realized he would never dance with me like he meant it. And I've had supposedly casual encounters, things that are supposed to be light and superficial, but instead reach their point M with a force and a weight and a meaning that leaves you pondering them for years, like a stone you keep in your pocket and keep pulling out from time to time to turn it over in your hand, wondering how something so small can feel so heavy, why it stays with you, how it manages to catch the light in just that inexplicable way.

For instance on the J Church streetcar down Market Street at midnight, I keep coming back to the smell of his cologne on my hand, my hand on the back of his neck, wondering why two lines that intersect so powerfully at one point in time always invariably continue to diverge afterwards, until some distance away from the point of connection it is as if no connection had ever occurred. I can no longer see his face in my mind, hear the sound of his voice, and by morning even the cologne has worn away. Two weeks later the event is only the idea of the event, as the mental pictures pixelate and blur, the tape wears through, and only the data firmly remain. We stood at such and such an angle to each other. The light came from over his left shoulder. At a certain point he said "Yes." At a certain point he closed his eyes. When we left we were moving in different directions.

These are the bits of information that remain in the file when form and color and sound and smell have been eroded. These things are the things I know but these things are not knowledge because knowledge exists at least partly in the senses and the senses never remember for long, do they? The mind attempts to remember what the senses told it. He stood here and I stood there. His beard was reddish brown, he was slightly taller than me, when I rubbed the back of his neck he seemed to lose his defenses a little. This is data but it is not memory. It is not a straight line to the past. It does not explain why this particular point M stayed in the files for so long, why it caused the mind to make so many loops and spirals around it when other moments were supposed to be more meaningful, took longer to arrive at, were so much more heavily favored in the betting. All that is left is the information that something about the particular intersection of your line and his was particularly significant, regardless of what it sounds like in the words you might use to describe it.

But we move forward through time, only forward, and so he is behind you now. Point Z is closer to you than he is now, because it lies in the direction in which you move. He moves in one direction, and you move in another, and the mind makes loops and spirals and crosses and somewhere outside of them is point Z, the place where it all makes sense or no sense, depending on what the letters spell when you line them up side by side, in their true and final order.

I ≠ AM

Where was I?
Where have I been?
Where am I now?

Am. What a curious word. I don't just I. I actually am. I have to keep amming each actual moment of I. No I without am, so I'm told, and yet I, in the secret places of its soul, remains possessed of a curious belief that it predates, and will outlast, am.

I don't am. I just I. When I forget to I completely, when I get distracted from the business of I, that's when I begin to am. Am is an illusion, and a confusion, because am is never sure, never satisfied, and it always wants something it can't have. When I forget to want things, it's because I've started to I again.

Am is a disease of I. A condition, a state of disrepair. A distemper, a bad humor. I is everywhere, am is somewhere. I is boundless, am is circumscribed, located, identifiable. I is utterly without characteristics or qualities. You can find I as easily in the cry of a bird or the motion of water in a glass as you can sitting behind a wooden desk or staring out a car window at a breeze moving through a field of wheat. Am, on the other hand, is easy to pinpoint and easier to describe. Am attracts modifiers like the sole of your shoe picks up gum. Am is hungry, or sleepy, or insulted, or afraid. And it never knows peace until it falls asleep long enough for I to cut the cord that binds it to am and go free, sailing over the tops of the houses, moving like a cloud through deep water, diffusing like a vapor in space.

Talking to Myself

So I'm talking to myself, talking to myself and I say: "Hi. What's your name?" And myself says, "If you don't know, I'm not gonna tell you." And I say, "Hey — why can't I ever get a straight answer?" And myself says, "Look. I wear the same clothes as you, I eat the same food, I brush the same set of teeth. When you look in the mirror, it's my eyes you see." And I say, "I know all that. What I want to know is: Who — the fuck — *are* you?"

My personal favorite episode of *Gilligan's Island* was the one where there was this giant spider that kept terrorizing everybody and taking the castaways hostage by trapping them in a little cave. The castaways tried to defeat the spider by rigging up a huge mirror on a bicycle, and then backing the spider into a corner by scaring it with its own reflection. And it was working until Gilligan broke the mirror — go, Gilligan. Anyway, I was thinking about this a while back and I realized that what this is, is a kind of modern answer to the Greek myth of Narcissus. And what it says is that instead of being attracted by our own image, many of us in this day and age are incredibly repulsed. And this is very true. I know that if anyone ever wanted to back me into a corner, all they'd have to do is show me an image of myself and I'd run till I hit the wall.

And then some wise guy in the mirror says, "You know why that is, don't you? You're not talking about yourself, you're talking about the way you see yourself. They're two different things. Why, if The Way You See Yourself were to call Yourself up on the phone and ask it out on a date, Yourself would hang up."

And I say, Good point, I think.

So I'm talking to myself, talking to myself, and I say: "Look, I don't understand. I never even knew you existed until I was almost grown up. And now you won't even talk to me." And myself says, "That's because you're afraid of me." And I say "Look, I'm not afraid of myself. I'm afraid of what I am when I'm not myself!" And myself says:

"Then why do you always break your promises?"

Look. Here's how it is. Once, a really long time ago, I was lying in bed trying to get to sleep, and I heard this loud knocking on the door. So I got up to go answer it, and when I opened the door there was no one there — I couldn't see a thing. So I go to get back in bed and when I get there, what do I see but myself, lying there in bed, just like I hadn't moved at all. So I say, hey, move over, I've really gotta get back in bed. And the other me looks up and says, "Oh, no. You'll spend the rest of your life trying to get back in bed with me, and it'll never happen until you figure out why you left."

So I'm talking to myself, talking to myself, and I say: "Look, this is ridiculous. I feel like we've gotten very far away from our original subject." And myself says, "I know. That's my point."

Big Glass Jar, or Pearls Go with Everything

I heard a story once about a woman who kept the ocean in a jar. A big glass jar like you might use for pickles or olives or something like that.

Woman. Ocean. Big glass jar.

She lived in a little plywood shack next to a huge empty wasteland where nothing lived and nothing grew.

Woman. Shack. Wasteland.

At night when she lay down to sleep she could hear the tiny creatures of the sea calling to her from the glass jar where they swam around and around in tiny circles, trapped by the clear walls of the world.

Creatures. Jar. Around and around. Woman in bed; no sleep, no sleep. There were sharks and octopi and plankton and whales, and starfish and stingrays and clownfish and seals, all swirling around like the sugar in your coffee cup, calling out to her in squeaky little voices:

Let us out! Help us! Let us out! Dorinda!

That was the woman's name. Dorinda. Sharks, plankton, starfish and seals, around and around, big staring eyes. Well, this went on until one night the tired, haunted woman rose from her bed and picked up the jar.

Throw us out the window! the sea creatures cried. *Throw us out the window with a smashing of glass!*

Sea creatures. Window. Big glass jar.

Smashing. Crashing. Big glass jar.

And the woman said: "I know how this goes. I throw the jar out the window. The jar breaks. Smashing. Crashing. The ocean is released into the wasteland which becomes its seabed. Sea creatures happy. Sea creatures free."

Woman. Ocean. Big glass jar.

"But if I let the ocean out of the jar, what's left for me? What do I have to dream about? What tiny voices will I listen to in the wee still hours of the night? Oh, no. I'd rather dream by the wasteland. By the dry barren wasteland with a head full of stingrays and seals."

Woman. Wasteland. Big glass jar.

Now the story I heard had more than one ending. I heard the story end more than one way. Sometimes the woman lived happily ever after, listening to the voices from the jar. Sometimes she gave in and let the ocean out of the jar, and in gratitude they crowned her Queen of the Sea Creatures, and built her a castle of coral and crab shells. But the ending I like best is the one where the creatures just kept swimming — around and around, faster and faster, night after night until finally the jar exploded and the water came pouring out, flooding the woman's shack, and the woman — who had been asleep at the time — was transformed into a school of plankton.

Happy plankton. Free plankton. Around and around.

Woman. Plankton. Big glass jar.

Snow

He had never seen the snow before. Where he lived it was always hot. The sun burned orange in the window as he sat at his desk writing; the sun's big orange face looked over his shoulder as he read the newspaper on a park bench. First thing he saw in the morning. Last thing he saw at night. The days were long where he lived. There was no winter.

He had never seen snow before, except in movies. It seemed impossible to him, that perfect crystals could drift down from the sky, so terrifically delicate and cold. It seemed to him that everything delicate melted in the heat of his life. Every perfect thought dissolved under the searing heat of the big orange sun. There was no tiny, immaculate thing that could withstand that touch. There was only dissolution, confusion, a drop of water where moments before the dream had rested.

But sometimes he would close his eyes and the snow would begin to fall. It came without being bidden, a fragile shower that drifted glittering from above. Sometimes he would close his eyes and watch the snow fall for a very long time. He would stretch out a hand and catch a single perfect crystal in his palm. He would practice the moment when he opened his eyes, trying to take the snowflake with him into the real world. He would try very hard to bring the delicate thing with him into the light.

For every action, an equal and opposite reaction. For every particle an antiparticle. For every truth a lie; for every dreaming a waking. One night the man fell asleep sitting up, with his palm stretched out. In a dream he stood up and undressed. He took off his pants, shirt, socks, underwear. He moved through his apartment opening windows, letting the cold air in from outside. He passed a mirror in the hallway, and he noticed that he was wearing a pair of glasses that he had never seen before. He took them off. Underneath there was yet another pair of glasses. He took those off as well. There was a third pair of glasses, and a fourth; and with each pair he removed, his reflection in the mirror became a bit blurrier, more diffuse, harder to make out. The image of him was melting away. The ninth pair of glasses were very small and difficult to see; he held them in his hands and they dissolved quickly, like snowflakes.

When the man woke up, the snow had begun to fall. It was falling gently everywhere in his apartment. It came tumbling down from the ceiling and little drifts had formed on his shoulders. The snow was falling gently past his field of vision, though he couldn't see it clearly. He couldn't see anything very clearly. But he knew how the tiny, perfect crystals must look. He had their perfection permanently fixed in his mind.

Talking to Myself: The Interview

Since the subject of this piece is myself, and my relationship to myself, it was very important to me that I actually interview myself in order to substantiate some of the claims I've been making, both factual and metaphysical, about him.

Unfortunately, he was initially reluctant to agree to the interview. Not, as you might think, because of his demented personal schedule or his fiercely protected privacy — face it, the man is a whore for media and a harlot for attention, and he always has time for an interview. Privacy? Ha! It is to laugh. He is an exhibitionist pure and simple.

The truth is that his reasons are quite personal and specific to me, and for a while I could not help but take them personally. It began to appear, quite clearly, that I am perhaps the one person or thing in the world that he is most afraid of. And this perhaps explains the sudden fevers and asthma attacks that would arise to cancel our meetings, the string of missed appointments due to nebulous, ill-accounted-for "emergencies" that always arose a half hour before we were to convene for the long-awaited, painfully elusive interview.

And how did I finally catch up with the man himself? I'm afraid it took a little bait-and-switch routine. You see, he reads the gay personals every week but he never responds to them because he's generally appalled at what he reads. The pissiness, the no-fats no-fems cruelty, the straight-acting-and-appearing hypocrisy, and worst of all the horrendous grammatical errors. "What monsters would walk the earth if gay men's faces matched their personal ads," he is fond of announcing. At any rate, I simply placed the ad I knew he was looking for:

> Russell Hoban reader, handy with tools and very
> good at math, seeks verbally devastating, epicure-
> an pansy with extensive collection of hard-to-find

```
CDs by various obscure British New Wave bands.
I'll listen adoringly while you expound on sub-
jects of esoteric interest, e.g. astrology, Irish
mystical poets,homoerotic themes in The Wind in
The Willows, and how very, very strange your life
has been, only pausing in my attention once in a
great while, just long enough to whisper sweet,
naughty things in your ear. Chubby men with asym-
metrical ears are a HUGE turn-on.
```

Well, of course he took the bait and in 24 hours I had a lunch date. When he found out how he'd been duped he had to laugh at my cleverness — after all, he is always willing to laugh at his own cleverness.

The meeting itself was a bit tense at first. There is...an awful lot of baggage. He feels, accurately I suppose, that I am not always the best influence on him. That I am at once his harshest critic and his worst flatterer. We agreed that the middle ground was something to be striven for.

He also admitted that part of his evasiveness came from a fear that I would reproach him for his failure to live the life that he — I — had imagined for myself. I told him that it was okay, because I had recently come to the realization — though I hadn't shared it with him yet — that I *am* living the life I imagined for myself. It's just that I don't always recognize my own imagination at work.

With anyone else but yourself, you can agree to disagree. But it was important that he and I make peace. I forgave him the grudges I've borne so long during that forty-minute lunch break; he looked so pathetic and helpless, and not at all the monster I make him out to be. So terrified of how he might be seen by others; so unaware of the signals he really does give off. Just for a moment, watching him hold forth on one of his daffy pet topics, I felt as if he and I were finally working together; as if, at long last, we had managed to leave the pair of us behind and move forward as one.

Night Diaries

Poems 1995-1997

January (The Routine)

The days are a slow poison and each
night is a teacup full of stars. Leopards of snow
on powderpuff feet stalk the countertops of my kitchen,
while blue moths mass and chant in the air above
my sleeping body. I rise and run through tunnels,
dodge pennies and iodine, and wake to drowse in a static
of dandelion fuzz and August daisies, each time and always
the same crop of dizzy, spinning eyes. Fall down a manhole,
drink the sleep of ghosts. Blink in a silver,
noiseless moment, no exits and no approach.
Eventually, I'll make a shopping list:
The buses will crouch in the streets like an army
of silent sphinxes as I pluck hungry suns
from the cold, electric winter sky.

Letter to Christopher

I leave my apartment at half-past eight,
half-asleep and half-unsure where I'm headed,
and why. The night is purposefully vague, cold, obscure,
and the various sources of light and patches of shadow
never collaborate to form a clear picture;
the buildings and the sky are saying nothing,
the books closed, the words erased.
There's a September-blue morning-glory
drowning on the sidewalk,
and my mind is full of the intricate patterns
formed by tiny pinpricks of light
against a chalkboard sky. I could give you a thousand reasons
why you and I don't know each other anymore,
and not one of them would mean a thing
if I were to see you now.
My book bag is heavy and its strap cuts into my shoulder.
I am thinking of your fabulous lover, the one with the thick
shortcropped hair, and the way he lays a casual hand
on your shoulder as if to say that you are his now,
and everything that came before him
was merely prelude and exposition. I need a haircut; my clothes
are wrinkled and fit me badly; I haven't bought a new shirt
in over a year. I wonder how many buses will pass me
heading in the wrong direction as another summer dissolves
and I stand on a darkened street corner,
scribbling poems in a notebook.

At the Turning

I.

My windows are colder to the touch now
and my hands have shriveled up like
brown leaves, shopping bag paper,
and the spiders whistle dark Russian melodies
from their webs, high in the corners of the bathroom.

II.

Yesterday, as I was talking to Tom, the video clerk,
he absent-mindedly adjusted his T-shirt and gave me a glimpse
of the soft red down on his stomach.
Outside, the sunlight was weaker and the trees were turning red
and the whole bus ride home, I thought about
Tom's stomach and the red trees rustling
in the still, cold afternoon. At home I drank raspberry tea
and went to sleep for 13 hours.

III.

The sunflowers sputtered and went out,
doused by the wet fingers of September.
The black-eyed susans and the tiger-lilies crumbled to dust
in their sleep, and the morning-glories froze
like innocents turning blue in a blizzard.

Somewhere you were thinking of me
and I was thinking about the geese scattered like
pepper-specks across the sky, and the geese
weren't thinking of either of us, their shadows gliding
across lakes and railroad tracks
and farmhouses; they think of nothing
because they are headed in the right direction.

Letter (4/24/96)

Night coy and vulnerable falls prey to the
cologne-heavy charms of the yellow sulphurous
streetlamp. The hard dull concrete reflects
the strange luminosity of their union, and
the early spring air is full of the dreaming
minds of city dwellers, which having fled
the skulls of their owners like so many crepe
paper bats flutter in late April confusion among
bare branches and power cables. Listen to
the hush and hum of the traffic, the urban
tides lapping against oily shores. There is no
sleep in the city, only dormancy. No darkness, only
shadow, and the heavy slate-grey lid
of sky that tells you there is nowhere to
go, go back to bed, go back to your artificial
unoblivion. But you don't. You swarm like a
nightflying insect, you buzz and obsess, you rise
till you burst and rain down across the city
like a powder of desperate metal.

Film Loop #12

Adrift on the grand seas of night,
your tiny toothpick bed carries you doggedly on
through tempest and lull;
each rolling, ruby-colored wave of sleep
takes you further from day and its demesnes.

Dutifully you are borne
through terrible straits and passes;
in forgotten continents you pay state visits
to the Teapot King
and The Hierophant of Windowpanes,
taste unknown fruit in tense, lachrymose
orchards; cross immense plains
where herds of tiny rhinoceros darken the sky.

And with each league and fathom you come closer
to the source of that old sadness you shield
your mind from by day;

Till you land each night on the shores of that country
hidden from waking eyes,
approach the same brilliant hedge,
stretch out a hand and prick your finger
on the same unreasoning thorn;
raise your hand to your mouth as always
to taste the blood of the past.

Cameo (March, 1995)

He offers me the small sweet onions
of his companionship
I kiss his eyebrows while the mantises
and beetles of spring watch hushed
    through the skylight
water drips from the ceiling pipes
and dim stars hammer the window glass
    above
I am aware of tiny, faint sounds
below the level of hearing
the scratching of microscopic violins
the whirring of the tiny wheels that move
the film forward
    as my hand moves across his chest
and the succession of tiny singular moments
    in which the rough feel of his chin
      the cool air and darkness on our bodies
and the temporary impoundment of past and future
    tenses from the vocabularies we use
seem to coalesce
like sounds into sense like words into nonsense
    and as we stand up
    amid scattering moths and distant arpeggios
I reel backwards from the long glance down
into the mind's oubliette

Night Diary #3

First, you staked me to a patch of sweet dark soil
and soaked my feet, left me alone as the wheel of stars
swung up above our heads, wiped your shoes
and went back inside the house.
All night long I though of you and grew, leafy and long
and strange, while the insects fiddled and the stars whistled,
leafy and long and strange. My arms stretched and twined
toward your window, making their way in spirals
and crosses to the place where you lay breathing, deep and even.
But day came and froze me in my place with light
and frost, and you came out and saw my night's work,
cut off my arms without a word,
pruned me back to a demure and simple shoot.
Night came back, I knit my brows and grew.
Leafy and long, silent and strange, and again I sent
my runners twining and questing toward your bed.
And this time my vines encircled you, and you woke
moments before the dawn: in time to see the tips
shrivel and shrink, the sweet red flowers wither
and close. And you hacked and you cut and you pruned,
still in your nightclothes, all that long cold morning,
till I was once again a simple bare stalk.
And you didn't sleep another night in that bed.
I have surrounded the house now,
overgrown it and ivied and carpeted it;
it is mine now, my keep and quarter,
and my mighty vines
have embraced that empty bed into ruins.
I guard the house now, with a patience I cannot express.
I wait for you to come back.

Axolotl

Aye-ayes and axolotls solemn at my birth
in the cooling cave where clay broke clean:
With orca eye and painted sway,
the puppet told my passage.

I emerge unshod to blink and shy,
moth-blind and half unmade.
Fifty moons and the whistle's fire
attend the rising cry:
a syrup of shadows and vinegar,
chiaroscuro of my uncertainty.

Aye-ayes and axolotls present
to measure the rising of my blood.
Quagga snort and ocelot cry,
fine cracks through the armor of heaven:
In the metal of my compassion
I kill days and dreams of days.

Aye-ayes and axolotls attend my wedding,
in the nether dell where beam nor bone
can come without my say. He is pumice stone
and I the river's tension. In the heat of his hand
I nothing am: the spring released, the skeleton
sprung. I guard all truths and hear all tales.
My nights are hawks and kraken song.

Fifty moons and the whistle's fire.
Yet our animal heaven
rusts with time, the clockwork
balks, the sinews stiffen. He walks slow,

and sight perpetually softens. The diamond
quarrel finds its mark, a tooth that drinks
greedy from the well of seasons.

Aye-ayes and axolotls mark
the draining of my pond.
They come as the ocarinas ebb
and the lilies burn with
autumn dry. He falls into the silent
trench: I follow sometime later.

Flower of chalk and the tattered edge
where leaves surround the sky:
a cluster of silent, fearful things.
With orca eye and painted sway,
ready for my conduction.

Aye-ayes and axolotls for my requiem,
they guide my soul
through the brush and the bright. We
navigate by mirror sense
where none but the animal
pass without their say.

Night Diary #2

I know where you are because
silly you, you forgot to cut that cord
that bound us years ago, before you moved
on. And even halfway across the world,
when you turn over in sleep
the springs inside me squeak. Your mouth
is partly open, even now: Your breath escapes,
tiny ghost of you, and comes to me as I lie awake
and whispers stories of you and what you do,
who you know, where you go. I send it back
when it's talked itself out, with small
coins and presents to hide about your person,
under the floorboards of you or the loose earth
behind the barn,
guilty windfalls you'd never suspect the origin of.
You'd never get through the day without
the things I send you, though you'd never dream it.
And how many wooden boxes have you opened?
How many worn ribbons have you tossed
away over your shoulder?
How many hills of earth stand between
you and the place where the sun rises,
drawn by horses of earth and blood,
horses that come a bit closer each night
to cresting the horizon of your sleep?

Night Diary #7

This house is matchsticks and mud
and I don't care. I move through it eyeless
and numb, tripping over rabbits and
pothos vine, while a tornado of spiders
and eggshell moves from room to room
collecting evidence, dusting for
prints. The child runs in, slamming
the screen door, raising a ruckus
as always: asking me if I've seen
the fluorescent explosion of sky outside.
I have, of course. But I prefer to stay
inside. I've already been a child once
and I didn't like it; besides,
they stole my bicycle long ago,
and sold it to the worm who now
sleeps beside me,
alone in his cave of teeth.
If it weren't for the coming summer,
I'd never want for anything:
never look out of windows,
never picture the bed galloping
away with me in it,
across fields of golden clover
with a crown of bees to protect me,
healed and shriven and free
in the forgetting light of spring.

Lay of the Antimuse

Ring me the knell of the hiccuping idiot,
tear out the tongue of the celibate scribe;
devour with silence his cries and his canticles,
marry the dark to his eyes.

In the moldering cell of the blessed apostate,
fathom me down to the nock of his thought —
poison the impulse, garrote the delivery,
strangle the seminal, blistered and taut.

Bury his blessings and unmake his elegies,
choke the grim deeds of his gravest desire;
let him weep in a circle of straining uncertainty,
cough in the dust of a counterfeit fire.

I will regard him, and safekeep and render him,
I alone secret him, twined with my roots:
When he sleeps at the end of my fugue of destruction,
I'll pay him in silver and gild him in suits.

The Desires of Glass

Poems 1987-1995

I Am the Man Vermeer Painted Over

Radiographs reveal me, standing framed in a doorway,
according to a placard at the Metropolitan
Museum of Art. My outlines unseen in the space
behind *A Girl Asleep*, I coalesce from elemental
twilight to keep my watch.

No one relieves my thankless routine, no
second shares my duty. Hour into century
I move through the silent house, tuneless, ephemeral,
the light on the polished floor my mansion,
the drafts in the hallways my demesnes.
I walk with you through the terrible peace
of darkened rooms, the warm quiet of a summer night,
the dusty stillness of a Sunday dusk,
among the lamps and the tables, the fearful solitude
of cups and glasses. Is your heart
breaking? Does your flesh dream the touch of
a stranger's hand? Is the clock too loud, does it frighten you
sometimes? When you wake, do you feel out of place? It is only
because you do not see me
that you are troubled at all.

I am there not there, now there now gone,
I am between the folds of the curtain's curtain;
future memory forgotten, question not asked.
I watch from behind the paint. I will know you
again in death.

Stitching a Dummy

With the eyes of mice
and the teeth of trees,
in the city of dreams
and the age of disease

we move through a chaos of butter and lies,
we survive in the silence of turtles and flies
and when we awake from our days under glass
we sleep without dreams in a field of dead grass

I'm waiting for light on a horrible night
and some shade on a horrible day
I'm waiting for truth in a 12-oz. glass
and a dream that will drive me away

I wanted to tell you a vision I had
the sky was on fire and the angels were mad
but I was imprisoned in a cardboard box
serving muffins and coffee to grandfather clocks

I wanted to tell you a dream I forgot
but my tongue was tied up in a Gordian knot
there were serpents with wings on a high green hill
and a music that gave me a terrible thrill

but the time for truth is nearly dead
and my tongue is sewn into my fabric head
so we live in the silence of turtles and clams
where the last frame sticks and the voicebox jams

and nobody knows where the lost things went
or how many hours the faithful have spent
waiting for a love that will penetrate their bones
like the voices of ravens, the spirits of stones

at the end of the movie
he turns to his friend
says I wanted to tell you
how things like this end

in the city of dust
and the age of disease
we think in our sleep
and we sleep on our feet and our knees.

Glass Insects

Ghostly, translucent insects
        scale the windows of the laundromat
where a hot, irritable clientele
        are spinning their clothes and sweating
I am exhausted
        having spent all day
riding around on slow buses
        which crawl down streets like
translucent insects on windowpanes
        (slow, methodical, mindless, unhurried)
trying to put my affairs in order
        so I can fly away to San Francisco
to soothe myself with grey waves and
        North Beach pizza, Berkeley bookshops,
multicolored Victorian hillscapes;
        and unsoothe myself with prurient
gatherings in darkness and light,
        shadow and motion
        (the distant brought near:
          terrible, dear),
a hint of danger, only barely restrained
        by the instinct for safety
like a hand that tugs you back
        from the railing
and the dark rocks below, the massive
        wet silence almost lost in
        obscurity, mystery,
          strange peace.

I am fetched from this contemplation
        by the dryers which have stopped

not because my clothes are dry
    but because they have used up my quarters
and wish to express their contempt for me
    I begin to fold the clothes and think
of this poem which I haven't yet finished
this old towel
    smells of salt and sweat
which reminds me of high school,
    locker room, phys. ed.,
a time of standing naked with my peers
    most of whom interested me
not at all,
    but a few, oh, a few—
made me know that I was separate
    the way the sun, in its heavy fire,
can make you know you belong on the ground,
    only there, to witness it,
different, awed:
    and this brings me back to the insects
whose numbers have only increased since I began,
    and whose bodies are only outlines,
transparent like the glass itself:

    glass insects, fragile,
endangering themselves because they know
    they are not the sun.

Laughing Sal

"Laughing Sal has been delighting tourists and scaring children
for well over fifty years now."
— *Sign on the display case of Laughing Sal, an antique arcade
attraction at The Musée Mecanique, Cliff House, San Francisco*

i

the voice of the iguana came
hissing softly in the blue china night
listen, it said, listen to the sound of explosions
soft explosions distant on the ghostly
sea-lit rocks littered with the bodies of
mechanical men and women and plastic camera casings

soon you will wake to dream
of dummies and coins
pink flowers that open and trees that twist slowly
in the black salty night

suddenly you awake with a clock ticking in your throat!

there is a ship on the rocks
and a fire on the heights

I cry out tangled in my sheets as the
lizard jumps in the aquarium and I
am slipping off the wet rocks
into the sea's cold music of starfish and seals

my lungs full of coins my eyes full
of laughing toy women,

robot wizards staring behind dusty glass

— a tiny execution scene —

> and outside the water, the black salty water
> crabs dance at the edge of the beach
> and the moon is coconut ice cream
> as I dream easy down to the pebbled floor.

ii

now it is the grey afternoon,
and the waves are silver lamé fabric draped
at the feet of the cliffs
which smile shyly in the pacific afternoon.
we're having french fries and a vanilla malt,
writing postcards, our heads full
of mechanical laughter and tiny purple flowers:

> "Dear Anne I have eaten nothing but basil
> for seven days now and the cypress trees really
> are amazing — but tell me: Wherever does one buy
> a gold lamé handkerchief?"

iii

my hands are purple with laughter
as I walk down Geary after midnight
haunted by your stubble, and these
strange new twists in my identity

the stars are hard, sharp, white
like teeth in the wet blue mouth of the night
and I am surrounded by a brilliance
I can barely absorb

"It's only money," he says,
                              " — people stuff it in my sock."

he buys me a small but exotic meal I can't finish, and
then we are wandering through
a summer forest of buildings taller than phantoms;

for the moment, nothing seems particularly
distinct from anything else,
as the robot dreaming under dust and glass
wakes to perform for the eyes and the quiet sea.

Map of the Body

If I could, I would make
a map of his body
as experienced by the mouth.
A map that could only be read by
other mouths. In order
to learn its secrets, you would
unfold the map, and press your lips
to it. And it would speak
of strength, of dignity and
mystery, of the hidden kingdoms
where a mouth could travel in rapture.
And as the mouth made its eyeless way
across continents of touch and taste,
it would pause from time to time
to marvel at the existence
of a map like this, that captured
so perfectly the blind amazement of
sex, a Braille of the erotic spirit.
Putting your lips to this map
would be as suddenly beautiful
as seeing him again after many years
had passed — and precisely as painful
as seeing him stand up, walk past you,
get off the bus; without meeting your eyes,
behaving as if he hadn't recognized you.

The Sideshow

This fear of the future tastes like burning rubber;
it is the face of a god covered with blood and semen.
I struggle through wet leaves and decay
into an odious noon, the wavering outlines,
the struggle for breath. The sun strikes me
with a peal of dissonant bells, catches my body
cowering like a drowning animal, a leper,
a pushcart vendor when the carnival is over.
My crooked shadow announces my presence,
my absence, my ridiculous shape
to the ground, the sky,
and the mass of confusion in between.

I have never wanted to be out in the open.
I prefer to be hidden from sight.

The past is a liar, the present a dull lover who will not leave.
I used to be in love with the future
but his threats of violence drove me away.
I have sometimes pined for the cologned promises of the past,
but soon it becomes like swimming when the limbs are heavy.
Now there is only the present, or the notions and the obligations
of him, and I am tired of his apathy, the weight of his body,
the odor of wine on his breath.
The trees are shimmering with ignorant joy.
I glance overhead to where summer airplanes split the sky,
remember day after day like this before;
reach for a symbol of transcendence as closure,
settle instead for an ordinary stop.

Summer Sketch

The summer icicles of an alien piano fill
my mouth with a silence like ripe strawberries,
the purple-gray surface of a closed window
on a Thursday evening. If I rose up like a
cloud of flies surrounding half a ripe cantaloupe,
startled by the soft claws and the prick of an
accidental recollection, a cantata of hungry
black and white piano keys would surround me
like a spiral staircase and peel away days of
dismal reflection to reveal the dormant wiring
of a winter introvert. Listen, the birds are melting.
The dim calliopes are chanting their doleful
celebrations of dried corn and yellow grass,
faded tiger lilies and asphalt. And huddled among
the beetles and the auto parts, submerged in the
intricate chaos I've created to protect me from the
heat and the collapse of weary skeletons,
I know — even here, even now —
that the brittle winds
of late September are coming
to bury another dead king.

Staring at Orion's Left Foot

From a dusty, secondhand chair
on a back porch somewhere on Earth,
I am staring at Orion's left foot,
which is resting lightly on the head
of the shaggy apple tree in my back yard.
The apple tree doesn't seem to mind, and
Orion looks reasonably comfortable.
It's a cocky, charismatic pose —
can a constellation be sexy? The chair,
which I bought five years ago from a widower
named Mr. Stankovich, is made of wood, under
layers of dust; my cat, who is rubbing
against the screen door, is made of
flesh, bone, fur, protoplasm;
the chimes dingling on my neighbor's
porch are made of metal. Staring
at Orion's left foot, in the darkness drifting
softly back and forth, the
thing that will send you tumbling
is to realize that all of us —
dust, cat, chimes, bone, Mr. Stankovich's chair,
screen door, apple tree —
we all came from the howling center of a star, the
joyful rage of light inside
that glimmering foot. I am somewhat
proud to know that the chimes,
being metal, had to come from a
somewhat large and hot star; that
making the materials for
bones and cats, for that matter,
is not something a star does

on the first try, not like whipping
out a rough draft and hanging it right up,
not at all, it takes stages, like papier-mâché.
Staring at Orion's
left foot, I sense the inevitability
of return; my mind jumps forward to
a time when my atoms are once more
dissolved and excited in the
heat of some star, and I feel myself,
chair and all, ready to tumble through
space from my back porch into the long
fall between myself and Orion's left foot,
where it lurks so many billion miles away.

I am sitting, quite comfortably,
on Orion's left foot, staring down at
a tiny dreamer on his back porch somewhere
on Earth. I am remembering the future,
as Stephen Hawking proposed, and if he's
listening, the future is papier-mâché,
is cats and chimes and dusty chairs,
is a gaze locked between a human and
a white blaze of light, across
billions of miles without awareness
of up or down, within or without, before
or after. The future is the unnoticed sound
of claws scratching on a screen door,
and little patches of darkness clinging
to the leaves of an apple tree, in my
backyard somewhere on Earth.

Nocturne

When we were young, younger
than we are now, we used to press
wine out of the darkness:
soft hands shaking we'd find the spot
at the base of the moon's throat,
at the foot of the old dead tree —
press awkwardly, burst the grape,
it tasted of blood and glamour,
melancholy and memory, the goldenrod
charge of libido and the strong
arms of the moon god's madness,
the singing of insects the footsteps
of guitars and dinosaurs — a torn
David Bowie poster — yes,
spirits between the earth and sky,
a conspiracy of trees and windows,
sexual angel crowned by midnight;
the sun murmured words through
caves of sleep and the ship came,
the enormous ship of your future
came looming in the night and you
were not afraid, you kissed the stranger,
you heard the angels, you closed your
eyes and you jumped.

Encountering Astrology
at The School Street Café, 1989
(In memory of Patrick Thomas Stack)

Sometimes it's impossible to tell
whether you've just been humbled
or elevated. It was a Sunday afternoon,
end of winter, silence of my soul
when I met Patrick, who
casually introduced himself
holding a mirror in his outstretched hand.

I saw a confused mess of stars, scars, snakebite,
concrete blocks; a city bird shaking its
dirty feathers in a patch of sun.
There was the sound of disturbed waters
and a match repeatedly being struck,
failing, going out. There was a map and a puzzle,
just the glimpse of something larger,
secret letters from self to self
and the first hints of a key to break their code,
a road of study and the beginnings
of a language, halting,
with which to speak. Names for
the compass points of confusion;
words for a preverbal knowledge
desperate to take shape.

And by the time I looked up
from the mirror,
Patrick was already gone.

prince of the forest

Owls blur seamlessly into the trees of sleep.
Unsparrowed slumber fathoms an illusionary king,
to a forest of feathers, and freedom,
and fear. Night is undivided, like sea ink
searching its way around obstructions
posed by a deadly smear of stars. He tall
as a ship of earth walks
in a puzzle of loud wood, he unimagined
moves without motion to speak without speech,
mesmers his rhythmic manifesto
into every crack and gap
between the bricks of the mathematical world,
mortar of kraken and mandrake,
fluid to fill the drowsy seams
between curtain and scene, and drown
the desert head. Among cities of foliage,
blind clouds of cricket prayer and
the spell of a smothered mushroom,
we follow him, iron dust to the
ferric wand, vagabond procession to the
hypnotic stronghold of sex and violets,
castle of drink and the eyeless joy:
unsevered union of scheme and sense,
rich earth perfume resisting
the guilt of the cities,
the ashes he buries.

Letter

Midnight presses an enormous face
to my window, dark fur and wet mouth
hungry for me like I am hungry
for vision or justice or
the "dear love of comrades."

In the silence between her paws
I drink silver from the mirror:
walk among the forgetful trees
with the dignity of windowpanes,
the charisma of a tall candle
on an evening in early spring;
a warm breeze causing trouble
in the attics of my desire.

I am a ship of blood and weakness.
Green eyes and soft bones
susceptible to the sound of my
own words, unsayable words
that bounce off my hollow walls
like sonar. And you,
you are the walls of the endless ocean:
No direction brings me closer,
no decision of mine will take you away.

Drowsing

Begin with the presence of soporific
dust in your veins, some
pixilated sweetness perhaps, or
a field of green dizzy space
behind walls of flesh but within a cold sense
of vertical internal sleep, not sleep
exactly but you are hanging at an oblique
angle from the walls of some café or other, warm
cinnamon winter smells, you are
expanding slowly through space like a
straw wrapper under the influence of a
few drops of soda

> ...you let go of the chains
> (in grade school you called this
> "bailing out")...

and have that delirious ritual sense of
being out of control,
inhabiting that impossible nowhere between
the swing and the end of the arc:
land in a crouch on the dirt bank

> — listen, does the beginning of the road
> exist at the same time
> as the end of the road?

or is one merely the culmination of a
process begun by the other, tree that
only falls when you witness the cutting;
there are stars imprisoned in my heart
when I think about it,
like fireflies in a jar —

the very thought of going from one
place to another makes me want to be
a maker of maps,
navigatory blackbird, or perhaps
the Queen's mathematician who falls
asleep and swims with dragons beyond the
bounds of the finite: makes me realize
the sky is asleep and only
in just those half-alert states do we
span the place between one place and another,
until we jerk awake and
it is left to the waking to
posit imaginary lands

Sonnet of the Sea Moth

Pinned uncomfortably between
    sleep and waking like someone
trapped between windowpanes,
    you vibrate with each confusing
wind that shudders the glass; it has
    the effect of cold water moving
through your insides, the sky purple
    and your melancholy red,
the sugar and the shiver —
    waking up without a compass to consult
you seek a reference point in your soul
    only to learn that

    all systems are down

perhaps your skeleton
    is the tree on which you are snagged,
unnatural anchor in the 3-D empire:
    This is why one end of you streams
toward darkness and the other light,
    one side toward clarity, while the
other is obscure. But you belong to neither
    or both at the same time;

perhaps you are
    the finger in the dyke, the stopper
    in the tub, the pin about to be pulled.

Suspended crazily between mountains
    above you and water below, you drift.

If you ever
    find the earth beneath your feet again,
journey awhile
    in countries of shadow
    and awhile in mountains of light,
undivided by the arbitrary hand of time,
    not forced to forsake one for the other;
you will be one in the two hands
    of truth, and the memory of solidity
    will no longer haunt you.
    Dreams will pass through you
    like starlight in moving water,
    like moisture in the thick summer air.

The Orchard
(for Ken)

I.

I see us in that old college house:
In my mind's unshakeable afternoon
you are surrounded by adoring
weedflowers grown just a little too high

on a day just a little too cold to wear
short sleeves and painted jeans
you've sketched a pair of glasses,
a clock, a window.

    Now it's time for English muffins and another
    English haircut band
    praising rivers and regret,
    solitude and the courage to cast
    a neat clean shadow
    and we do, believe me, we do

and now you have drafted
an immense confusion of globes,
unfocusing themselves in a conniption
of blood and pinkness,
gentle and angry, like the half-finished poem
    I find in the bathroom

    while I work in incense smoke
    and the faintly sweet bitters of
    youthful passion split off from the stalk

we have an attic full of frustrated ambitions
dusty and gleaming, we have
walls full of manic shadows, mysterious
dressers and mirrors, days ahead
full of vintage shirts, flooded streets and weeds

and in the afternoon light bats swoop and dive
in the air above the street where we live;
you sprawl on your back with a Jim Carroll book
and an ashtray made to resemble a tiny Spanish matador

and the light of our afternoon has this particular quality
I can't seem to capture with my net of words.
It is a sadness made slightly from rapture,
a transcendence made only of youth;
we are children writing the words of adults,
and adults given the forgetfulness of children.

II.

Something is accumulating like the
paint caked on the knife,
like the paint chips on the brown windowsill;
but for now a breeze of jasmine smoke is enough
to distract us. There are the mysteries
of sex and rooftops, that tall purple cloudshape stretching
arms across the sky

(his heavy form unknowable and brightly obscure
as he reaches out to you in a darkened classroom;
stories you tell me of equal parts wonder and fear,
explorer in a country of strange sacraments
withheld too long)

there is the inexplicable *sabi* of the Midwestern dusk
and the lure of conversations that butt up against dawn

but mostly it is given to us to be
seekers in a landscape of bodies and questions,
        chasing shirt-tail grails and the light of the sudden grin
        (a limbo of anticipation sweeter than its object):

we will not live this way for long,
but there are infinities to be crossed along the way.

III.

A few hours into evening I found
a sleeping mouse stiff in the closet

the world has stiffened lately
under a layer of snow, and
        since I am the only one in the house to witness
        the passing of a fellow hider,
        another burrower in the earth and the wood,
I make a small grave under the
Allen Ginsberg willow tree in the front yard.

        Winter and we retreat into our book of shadows,
        the inward spiral, Patti Smith records and
        books about Merlin, tea of blackberry,
        rosehips and dandelion root

        you grip the staff and peer at the bowl
        of flower petals and burning paper,
        say whatever words come to you,

think of his solid stare and moonlight on his chest:
  the least of our mysteries
  is as tall, as immense, as the world has hidden places

I picture you wading into a river of photographs
you've disowned, graduation pictures,
summer gangs in shorts;
you are defenseless, choking on
failed awe and deflated romance,
sneezing allergic, perversely amused —
your life produces fantasies, relationships and
involvements like a tree ritually offering leaves to the spring:
summer warms them, teases them with promises of heat
and glory, then autumn crumbles them with a sudden
sublime movement and you are left
staring at a halo of ice around the dead oak
in the yard, sulking in the snow in your deep
winter coat

you will retreat into the sanctuary of your bedroom,
the place where you hide and wait for the present to crumble
and reveal something more solid, waiting behind it.

A Trick of the Light

After the film is over you
sit very still almost as if
the flickering of the screen had
hypnotised you into believing
you were part of the film,
and now that the screen is blank
your mind is blank, your life is
empty and you are the ghost
of a ghost.

After the film is over you
sit unmoving, dreaming of
the cornflake girl or the space commander
with the sky-blue eyes and when the
test pattern finally appears it's like hitting
the ground after a ten-year fall.

After the film the crabheaded spider-creature
asks you to dance and you offer it your arm
which it accepts, carefully, with one delicately
extended claw, you
trip over its many legs and it helps you up,
clicking and gurgling, asking you if you come
here often, if you know where to find
the traitor Delaunay.

After the film is over you wonder
why you've never been to Venice,
why you don't speak French better,
why you never answer letters. After the film
is over the telephone rings,

more faintly than usual, and just for a moment
you make believe you don't know who
it will be when you answer, it could be anyone,
anyone at all.

After the film is over you stare at the screen in
disbelief, surprised and vaguely offended that the
sense of story could desert you so easily,
leaving you stranded in a world without a coherent plot.
You examine your own life critically, looking for
character development and continuity and the emergence
of a really strong hero or two and maybe a magnificent
underlying theme to tie it all together,
but all you see are words on the page, the dance
of random dots.

After the film is over I notice
you've fallen asleep on my arm and I
want to wake you up so I can go to bed,
but it takes more than that to break
the silence at the end of the journey,
to shake off the spell of someone else's story
and find the courage to face your own.
Sometimes it takes until morning.
Sometimes it takes your whole life.

Summer

Should soft red sparks come
groaning from your heart;
or soft green wind brush
breathing from your throat —
if great gold beasts
roar softly in your brain,
or the rain read quiet verse
curled up on the chair beside the lamp.

Should birds with tall long legs
eat chocolate cake,
while purple smears
from sky to slanting sea,
and Beethoven paints the evening
air with strings and reverie;
could autumn come and find the
fields in sleep already waiting,
and us behind the house, with rosehip tea.

When earth should turn a somersault
into the dizzy ether,
and birds, the eyes of night,
mistake the moon for angel cake:
Beneath the maple shadow
is a shadow made of breath;
between the hands of darkness
there is time.

the moment the body feels pain

The moment the body feels pain
is a long room without windows.
Standing in the center of the room
the floor stretches out miles behind you
and before you, a thousand-year
doom of linoleum. The doors are
not visible; sometimes, not even
the memory of doors.

We hold our sides and wait.
Think of moonbeams on ice;
think of bodies melting
easily like butter under
warm liquid sunlight.
Think of a ship that moves
continuously from one point to
another; without thinking,
without even a breeze to
stir its sails.

Lisa Goddamn

(for Lisa Buscani)

Some telephones are blue
but the best are red:
    red with love, red with dish,
    red with chatter
and the worldmad,
day-weary laughter of weeknight evenings.

Cooking something, spaghetti maybe,
    in the kitchen ahum with 8:00
    and electric lights:
I will phone you and make you stop.
Or my phone will ring
    and the soup will sputter, the
    ovensomething will die a long
    slow death,
because the dish on the phone
trumps the dish in the oven,
    always,
that's what friends are for,
to ruin the dinner with too much pepper
        and the vinegar wine
        of evening sarcasm —

Or perhaps it's Sunday afternoon,
and, in a triumph of the new
laws of causality
      which modern physics is only
      scarcely beginning to
      comprehend,
you will have been taking a shower

precisely at that moment because and
only because I phoned you
precisely at that moment

and for me you will drip
        like an alley dog under a raingutter,
because we have men to assassinate —
    the delightful ceremonial
    execution by sarcasm
                of various heads of state
                who have messed with the state of our heads,
                marinated in our aggravation,

till shaken in a batter of mirth
or sighing like a pushbutton hand dryer,
    we have jiggled and baked
    ourselves dry of our drippy realities.

This is our mission,
hand in phone in hand,
    to confront that ubiquitous
    kvetch we call the Ugly Truth;
and after grilling and gnawing
and fluffing and folding her,
        soaking her in the unexpected
        salt of the caught-off-guard tear,
we learn, somewhere
in the uncharted moments after
midnight —

She is us, buying cheap candy at the
Southport Osco, in a dark moviehouse,

having shared the taxi
    of empty Tuesday night streets,
our knees on the threadbare seats ahead of us:
Bette Davis in *All About Eve*;

The Ugly Truth is the electric shadow
we make together, the consummate celluloid
queen who camps despair into laughter
    and stuffs anxiety
    into a snug one-liner,
    drifting unfazed by the lonelier terrors
        across the screen,
    through the coffeed evening where
    she announces for us,
      for once and for all,
      "I — HATE — MEN"

...But we don't really, because
they're good for a giggle
now and then, after all;
    and the snow is waiting
    on our windowsills when we get home.

The Buddha Receiving a Gift
of Heart-Shaped Chocolates

You know very little about me now.
Not that I have a temper, for the first time in my life;
not the white shirt and tie I'm forced to put on every day,
or the way I carry twelve pounds of books in a backpack
on the off chance of getting five minutes to
read. You don't know of the dashing Ethiopian girl who
stole my hand to dinner last night, flashing an impossibly
English grin over huge plates of spongy bread and fava beans,
telling me about paraplegics and the history of a family
older than either of our troubles. You don't know that I
speak a bit of Spanish now, or that last night Gustavo
the dishwasher and I carried out the restaurant's garbage
together, and looked together for the evening moon,
and he told me that there was no moon, *"estrelles solamente,"*
and I understood him. And he patted my back and we walked in,
shaking our heads at the moon's desertion. You'll never know
of my first kiss taken in danger on a rooftop, or what my
apartment looks like with the lights turned low and an
Edith Piaf tape playing, or how I found myself after many
years of distraction in a series of science fiction novels.
Most of all, you don't know that I haven't loved you almost
a year now, and no longer make jokes when your name comes up.
I know now that you'll know nothing about me ever again;
until perhaps we should meet again in the space
where these lives end, and events become meaningless
as they were always intended to be.

Ban Sidhe Bridge

Through the redpenny ditches
of Ohio our spirits travel, backwards
to a time when our bodies were small
and the hum of the car made sense.

   Like this our Sunday drive
   brings us to the abandoned

   riverhouse; park in the grass lot
   up the mud slope and two small boys

   peel back the warped chicken wire,
   climb aboard the rickety structure, look down
   like careful Indians at the moving water.

Where the banshee has hidden in the afternoon mist,
the brown banks steal form from my mind
and only my teeth can hear the impact
of your firm and careful steps on the bridge.
My soft bones feel you walking ahead of me
and in the still silver mood
this wet day makes, I think I see your heart flashing
ahead of me like a bicycle reflector
on a brave summer evening.

My none-too-brave blood splashes against these banks
with a thick and liquid mutter. I know all the riddles
of this antique place — in my streams there's all the vagueness
I inherited from father Neptune. My feet make no creak on the
boards. Myself and the water, this is what we say:
Our strength is never in the moment, it can only be assessed
from the vantage point of centuries, like the rivers that
first gorged canyons from the monolithic world.

You, too, are deceptively passive, pushing slowly and
inconspicuously like the shoots of mighty trees. We grew
the oaks that built this bridge, our firmly gentle hearts
the tools of time.

> We climb carefully
> over the dried and splitting
>
> rails to sit on the lovely edge
> of dashing cold death —
>
> the damp wind infiltrates our jackets, puts
> an echo in our breath. Looking down to the dizzy
> stream, vertigo makes its way like a chillful tickle
> into my precarious manhood. We two wet and crazy
> boys discuss broken legs while the smoking birches
> build their still murals.

Our spirits glide in ripples over the slick
mirror below: My mouth opens slightly, the little wind
escapes my lips. My copper-haired ghost takes its slippery stroll
around us, slides through the woods in a silent act of memory,
as the leaves wrap their quiet teeth around my feet;
damp shapes and a wet smell,
loaves of bread smoking in the forest.
Mirrored years slip by softly, mumbling on the wet rocks
below the bridge. Look down, through the slats
to the graveled water. You, my comrade who
brought me here, are the only sound the bridge
makes in the steel chill of the tumbling world.

I'll bury my heart in the embankment,
cover it in a grave of leaves, carve our names in the
wood to make you remember. You'll come back to water the
ground with each new season, till wild flowers bear
nectar from the sugars of my blood.

The State of My Life
(*for Jane*)

I could get down about it but
fortunately I have a sister who
visits from time to time
    bringing Gordon Lightfoot tapes
    and cedar-scented shirts with
            deep green stripes,
            natural soap and
            maroon ostrich feathers
   leaves quietly in the morning
            before I wake
   with only the
   Ultravox record on the coffee table
      to mark her passing

only the grace of god enables us
to stumble into the gifts of a sister, or
    dinner with someone who really appreciates
    something made entirely from avocados
and by this we are partially healed

Van Gogh

Sometimes when I find myself
wearing this funny balloon of flesh,
I find it necessary to go walking
in a still place of tilled and vaulted earth,
the fingers of whose trees suggest god;
the wings of whose sparrows
beat accidental haiku
in flashes of black motion
and tiny heartbeat;

If you've finished your soda
put down your glass
and perhaps you'll accompany me
into a day of blurred wind
and confused sunlight,
which seems to indicate
that we are crooked and delicate
and that it is especially beautiful to be
crooked and delicate
in these daft cages of imperfect flesh —

And if I take you among the solemn trees
that inhabit this old place,
promise you will hear the leaves mutter,
promise you will see the water dropping,
promise you will feel the wind
folding around us like origami paper;
promise you will see the way the night
hangs crooked and naïve in the sky.

My blood fills with chlorophyll;
my feet are light as stone
and twice as quick.

Now, my companion of days,
speak to me suddenly with a breath
full of tiny shivering lights:
Promise to see the wind without reason,
the thought in the tree stem,
the movement in the wooden body,
jagged and slowly ecstatic —

Promise to breathe beside me
in that cold electric way:
We are young,
and near enough to heaven
to feel the confusion of joy that fills
our legs and our chests
and our heads,
to see the way the sky hangs panting
in quick awkward strokes
of purple and frenzy.

two poems appassionata

i

I want to outrun Beethoven's music;
run faster than the piano can sweep.
I would not do this with legs, or breath,
or speed: I would do it
with the instantaneous purity
of a straining, dark contradiction.

ii

You are Beethoven in the dark; clattering
my nerves like the lovely noise of the piano.
You violate my arteries with an angel's confusion;
a bliss of senses destroyed, and remade into the opposite
of awareness. The sweat of the soul's surface; anticipation
made holy, carved figures that move in a distress
of wings, strings, negativity and desire. The chord
you've sounded disturbs the earth's flesh itself;
the sea recedes like sleep, a deadening energy
that numbs and comforts. Alone, I vibrate in darkness.

The Octopus

My sister used to love the Octopus ride at the fair,
the big black thing with the arms
that threw you around in a way that seemed to defy
all order. Shaken up as we were, we liked to get shaken
up more, though I stuck to the Tilt-a-Whirl generally.
The Octopus had too much visible machinery for me,
grease and cables and metal that seemed to imply
that it was all based on a system, and even then
I had, I think, an instinctive distrust of systems —
systems that might kill you if they break down on an
unlucky day. It would be years before I would discover chaos
theory, and find written validation from the world of physics
of what was then only a gut instinct — if it works, eventually
it will break.

Better not to have to see the machinery, I thought,
better not to worry about the system;
better to believe it was all circus magic.
With the Tilt-a-Whirl, all you saw were
the little red cars and the circles, the little circles you moved in
within the larger circle, and after being flung around
in the chaos long enough it would start to explain itself to you
by making you shut your eyes and forget about
things making sense.

Years later, now more than ever, I find it necessary
to shake the order out of my mind when I'm thinking too much
about physical systems, and the danger of breakdown.
So the other night, when my friend Amy came in her dark car
that rushed us through the disorderly night,

I was thinking about
the powers of motion to soothe disturbances —
speed, smooth speed seeming like the answer
to a question about fear
(or maybe not an answer so much as an easy lie,
thinks the worrying mind:
a lie that holds until the impact comes and the wreckage,
the sirens, the flames that prove that nothing
goes smoothly forever, after all).

So I got in the car, and we drove to a nearby fair,
to climb aboard the greasy machinery,
and take a chance on systems of motion that might not end in
wreckage; because being sped through the air
on a summer evening is good,
and with eyes closed the insistence of motion makes one
forget about the possibility of accident, at least on the surface.

And again and again we climb aboard machinery
designed to rush us through the night
in patterns of speed and confusion:
as if we were not already moving in patterns
of speed and confusion,
as if we were not each the disintegration of a pattern
in the uncertain precession of night.

lughnassadh iii

Westward of heaven,
there lies a dim country
of rose and gold
where trembling images collide.

There would be found yours and mine:
silent as mirrors, nervous as lead.

I dread you,
as I dread the rosegod—
the kiss of nepenthe in Arcadia;
picture a bending prince uncertain,
wavering in the grim distance of time.

There are no flowers that do not ache.

Love gnaws like the mandibles of hell:
speaking a brace of rusted promises,
sewn with a delicate edging
of fouled time.

Dodging words and eyes
leaves me little energy to think,
to destroy the dance that twines our trails.

There is no lightning that does not burn,
no bending that does not strain;
no touching you without
the cold knowledge of moonlight, pulling me away:
I am wet and immersed in a thunder
I cannot see.

essays on distraction

Whatever seamless quality of perseverance
holds the rain together
must hold me together as well: gutters and trimmed windows
and the pointed roofs of houses,
the changeless gables of Victorians exquisite,
sitting momentless in the wind
— speaking of blue rain, a brush of thoughts,
a warm remembrance moving softly through the hair.

Whatever keeps the rain from crying as it weeps —
the sadness of water held from breaking apart
by some grateful concept of
the wetness of being, blurring vision, a sudden holding together
letting it run down windows while moments tick away —
whatever keeps the wind from moaning as it speaks
must keep me from breaking as I fall, as well.

Wherever souls fly to get warm —
what palaces of crystalline unconcerned thought
secure their troubled hearts in eternity,
making them relax and unclench their dreading eyes,
immersing them in rivers and nursing them in the denial
of day's warrior unconcern
          (till they open slowly, gratefully,
          like an image of roses under water)
— there I must be flown as well.
Somewhere where the rain is unspeaking
and the wind is loud without pain:
when you speak to me but find no presence,
only my eyes going still as crystal, sparkless, elsewhere —
locked in a moment with no beginning or end.

Letter to Carl Jung in Vienna

When the first Apollo rocket landed on the moon,
Carl Jung was on it. It has always been his territory,
that sea of dreams; like moths struggling in a thick wind,
we walk subsumed in dust as we struggle
to take a conscious step.
But our feet move on in sleep: Jung knew that goddess,
the lady of somnambulism, who drifts about reasonlessly
beneath the sharp waves. I caught sight of her gown once,
fluttering by my bed shortly after midnight —
I wasn't supposed to be awake, and to this moment I wonder
if I've been fully awake since. Lunatics in dust shout at me
from bus stops, of the death of my mother
and worse things: Carl Jung, your experiment has not ended.
I have been waiting for "one raptured glance" from the sun
longer than moths have spoken to patient men;
I have burned my skin to peeling without hope of getting warm.
Fire-the-symbol deserts fire-the-manifestation just
as the victim leaps headlong into the fierce flower
of heat; leaving us empty-handed and foolish,
as if we'd been chasing reflections.

Sonata

My window startles a church steeple and a moon conversing,
the steeple speaks puncture, bursting, the moon shy
as all moons are shy turns away, hides its head,
runs to a different room. I often catch that
expression on its face, the uncomfortable pretense of being
a round thing and vulnerable in a sky full of pointed
objects, stars sharp as tacks, threatening buildings
that rise like a grunt of aggression from the sodden
countries below.

I am a round thing now in a room full of steeples;
some would say I am begging for the puncture.
The way ripe cherries beg, the way full balloons suffer
in silence for the anger of the pin. Some
things just need to be provoked.
I'm leaving this room, before I say something else
glib and incomprehensible about
ripe tension, fruit, the mechanical film movements
I'm sensing; someone stop me before I'm out the door.

Coiled in a bare room, rising in the window,
the dim haunted blue blushing outlines
that diffuse into a jagged voice both
visual and tactile, no, odd.
The moon changes color, size, heat, it sweats
and I sense it emoting, but one thing never changes:
There is always a moment when it turns its face away.
The moment when you get up from the bed, shutting the door
behind you like a cat's silent tail
as if to end the evening;
the moment I lose sight and think, balloon;
blundering for something to pop me, quick, I am huge
and cannot bear to take up space another second.

Notes

Photos: Front cover, clockwise from upper left: the cliffs at Dun Aengus on the Isle of Inishmore, Ireland; Glastonbury Tor; Laughing Sal; sign by the rocks near Cliff House, San Francisco, 1986; beach near the Joyce Martello Tower at Sandycove, near Dublin; "pineapple" photo of author, promo for *Talking to Myself*, 1997. Back cover, top: The Callanish I stone circle on the Isle of Lewis, Scotland. Below: the author at the Avebury stone circle in England. (Photo credits are given at the front of the book.)

What the Sea Means

"Zeppo" — *Arthur*: Harpo's given name was Adolph, later changed to Arthur.

"Tommy El" — *The Oulipists*: The Oulipo (*Le Ouvroir de Littérature Potentielle*, "Workshop of Potential Literature") was a group of writers and mathematicians founded in the 1960s. The Oulipists argued that at the beginning of a text, the possible choice of words was too great and would overwhelm the writer, so a set of rules was necessary to reduce the possibilities. Original and provocative content would be created as a by-product of rigorous form. George Perec's novel *A VOID*, written entirely without the letter e, is probably the most famous use of Oulipist technique.

"The New Planet" — *Sabi*: Derived from a word meaning "lonely" or "solitary." The term *sabi* is used to refer to a poetic atmosphere frequently evoked by the Haiku master Basho, in which one is aware of the smallness and fragility of life viewed against the impersonal vastness of the larger universe.

"Moth Song for a New Summer" — See note under "Letter to Carl Jung in Vienna" in *The Desires of Glass*.

"Letter to Mark in Dublin" — *Seventh house*: In astrological charts, the house of one-on-one relationships (lovers, enemies, business partners, etc.)

"Critique of the Geometrical State" — *Ouroboros*: the alchemists' symbol of the serpent devouring its own tail.

"Glastonbury" — The town of Glastonbury in the southwest of England, associated with the Isle of Avalon in Arthurian and Grail mythology. Its most striking feature is Glastonbury Tor, a 150-meter mound that rises above the town. At the top of the Tor, part of the ruined Chapel of St. Michael still stands. In Arthurian times Glastonbury was surrounded by lake waters, appearing as an island. Legend says that Joseph of Arimathea brought the Holy Grail to Glastonbury; one tradition holds that a holy thorn tree sprang up where he struck his staff in the ground. In 1191 monks at Glastonbury Abbey excavated a coffin containing the remains of two humans, under a stone slab with the inscription (in Latin) "Here lies buried the renowned King Arthur in the Isle of Avalon." Though it's impossible to say whose remains were actually found, it's been established that the excavation did take place. The Chalice Well, a natural spring near the base of the Tor, is said to have sprung up at the place where the Grail was buried. It's surrounded by beautifully maintained gardens and was the site of alleged miraculous healings in the 19th century. Yet another tradition holds that prior to the Abbey, Glastonbury was home to a Druid college with a "perpetual choir" that chanted night and day.

"Bestiary: Zero" — ...*Swan once observed by Rilke*: As described in Rilke's poem "The Swan." (I recommend Stephen Mitchell's beautiful translation.)

"Tara" — The "Camelot" of Ireland, Tara was the seat of the High Kings of Irish legend; to rule Ireland it was necessary to be recognized as rightful King of Tara. Originally a Neolithic ritual site, with a variety of earthworks including a small passage grave. It's located in County Meath, not far from Dublin.

"Notes from first trip to San Francisco..." — *The spiral dance*: ceremonial dance performed at Wiccan rituals. Participants form a circle holding hands, and the human chain moves in a leisurely spiral toward the center, at which point it doubles back and spirals outward again, allowing those moving inward and those moving outward to greet each other, face to face, as they pass. *Laughing Sal*: See note on the poem "Laughing Sal," in *The Desires of Glass*.

"Avebury" — Located in Wiltshire, England, the Avebury stone circle is the world's largest remaining stone circle in terms of diameter (1401 feet) and number of stones. It's now divided into four sections by roads, and many of the stones are missing (destroyed or buried); but the remnants are still spectacular. Its beginnings date to about 2600 B.C.

"Callanish in August" — The Callanish standing stones (or Calanais, to use the Gaelic spelling) are located on the Isle of Lewis, in the Outer Hebrides off the coast of Scotland. The largest and most famous stone circle on the island is Callanish I, where poems i and ii of this suite are set. The stones are composed of glittering Lewisian gneiss. There are also a number of smaller stone circles on the island including Callanish II, III and IV; poem iii in this suite was written specifically about Callanish IV, a smaller and somewhat harder-to-find circle. As opposed to other, sun-oriented stone sites like Stonehenge, the positions of the Callanish I stones are thought to mark the movements of the moon rather than the sun; the solar imagery in this suite occurs because I visited Callanish on Lughnassadh (August 1), the Celtic holiday marking the ritual death of the sun god and beginning of autumn.

"Immense Buddha Under Fire" — Written after the Taliban's destruction of the Bamiyan Buddha statues in early 2001.

"The Writer's Prayer" — Staged in *Too Much Light* in 1999, with the cast in a circle on the floor holding unlit candles. At the start, the candle at the 12 o'clock position is lit, and the person holding it then lights the candle of the person to his or her right. The candle-lighting continues counterclockwise until all candles are lit. Two voices then speak the text in unison. At the end of the piece, the candles are blown out one at a time, again moving counterclockwise.

"Dooncarton" — The Dooncarton stone circle is named for the nearby village of Dooncarton in county Mayo, Ireland. Dooncarton is apparently small enough that it wasn't marked on our driving maps; I'm not certain whether we even saw the village itself. We only found the circle by following directions from stonepages.com (an indispensable site for megalith maniacs). *Beloved, gaze in thine own heart*: from Yeats' "The Two Trees."

Big Glass Jar

"The Idea of You" — Performed as a solo monologue many times, and staged in *Too Much Light*, in 1991, as follows: At the top of the piece, Phil Ridarelli and I are seated in two chairs on stage, back to back. After the words "...but lately, you were beginning to confuse me," Phil rises to stand beside his chair; on the line "I nobly stepped aside" I rise to stand beside my chair. The piece ends with the two of us regarding the empty chairs.

"Young Person's Guide to Synchronicity" — The *Too Much Light* CD recording of this play adds some repetition of words not given here. Staged in *Too Much Light*, in 1992, as follows: Greg Kotis begins drumming on a cardboard box, in darkness. A spotlight comes up after the drum intro and I begin speaking the text over the rhythm. At the point in the story where the man reads from the book, a spot comes up on Ayun Halliday who reads those lines, from "June 17th:" through "...unhappy childhood." Her light clicks off, and I resume the text. On "its eyes would be blank" Greg stops drumming; after "Like two empty marbles" my spotlight clicks off.

"A Poverty of Murk" — Staged in *Too Much Light* in 1993, for four voices. Each of the four cast members spoke one of the paragraphs of the text, in succession, lit by a single light bulb. The bulb was unscrewed after each speaker finished, to create a quick blackout, and then the next cast member screwed the bulb back in to light him or her self before speaking.

"The Day of Your Return" — Performed in *Too Much Light* in 1990.

"Story #423" — Staged in *Too Much Light* in 1992. I delivered it standing in a spotlight, leaning slightly at an odd angle and clutching three small balloons.

"Between the Lines in 4/4 Time" — Staged in *Too Much Light* in 1995, as follows: I sit in a chair stage left and deliver the main part of the text. Phil Ridarelli and Scott Hermes sit in chairs side by side, stage right. Scott speaks the line "Hey, let's practice our dance steps" and they stand up and begin doing an awkward box step together. They stop dancing on the line, "Every now and then one of my straight friends asks me..." Phil says, "Tell me, Dave..."; Scott says, "That must have been hard..." They then resume dancing in a close-dance embrace as I finish the text.

"Jimmy, Roger & John" — Staged in *Too Much Light* in 1995; three cast members lit me with hand-held instruments to create varying shadow images on the back wall as I delivered the text.

"Told Me What?" — Circa 1994. Generally delivered as a simple monologue with no special staging. At the time this was written, Rush Limbaugh's *See, I Told You So* was still leering at the world from bestseller racks.

"Freedom (for Chuang-tze)" — Written and performed in *Too Much Light* shortly after Bill Clinton's inauguration in 1993. I delivered the text sitting on the floor of the stage, speaking over the recorded sound of water in a stream playing softly. In the months prior there had been much news coverage of the forcible repatriation of Haitian asylum-seekers. Regarding the title: The Taoist philosopher Chuang-tze was once approached by two officials sent by a prince to offer him an administrative position. Chuang-tze mentioned a famous sacred tortoise, kept enclosed in a chest on an altar, and asked the officials whether they thought it would rather be dead and venerated, or alive and wagging its tail in the mud. When the officials made the obvious answer, Chuang-tze replied, "Begone, for I too would wag my tail in the mud!"

"Painting for an Empty Canvas" — Performed in *Too Much Light* in 1993, the week after the bombing in question. I stood next to a screen on which an empty square of light was projected. This piece was written two years before the first time I ever heard the words "World Wide Web;" if it had been written five years later I might very well have been able to find one of Leila Al-Attar's paintings on the Web somewhere, and written a somewhat different piece.

"Parts of Me Function Like a Dream" — Written as the opening to Spin 1/2's 1994 show of the same name. Accompanied by a light-hearted Alex Christoff musical theme. The words in capital letters were on placards held up by other performers. In the case of the "PARTS. PARTS. FUNCTION..." refrain, the words were on separate cards, tossed aside Bob Dylan style. In performance this text was shortened somewhat due to time constraints; this is the "author's cut."

"City Dream #8" — Another piece from *Parts of Me Function Like a Dream*. Accompanied on stage by a dreamlike Christoff composition and delivered next to a black-and-white film of the Chicago Loop landscape by Armando Vasquez.

"Please Drive Slowly" — Written for *Parts of Me Function Like a Dream*, and subsequently performed in *Too Much Light* as well; in both shows delivered standing next to a slide of the sign shown on the page.

"An American Childhood" — Performed in *Too Much Light* in 1993. The title is swiped from Annie Dillard, though she's not to blame for this burst of dementia. The text was delivered as voiceover, with a stage picture featuring Lusia Strus on her hands and knees, reflectively scrubbing the stage using first a brush and then eventually her long blonde hair.

"Justice Takes a Roadtrip Part II" — Performed in *Too Much Light* in 1995, delivered standing next to an empty chair in a square of light. Written shortly after a jury spared Susan Smith the death penalty; she had drowned her two children in a car and blamed a fictional "black man" for the crime. At the time this piece was performed, David Protess's NWU students had not yet freed the Ford Heights Four and re-ignited the national debate on the death penalty. The original *Justice Takes a Roadtrip* was a piece by Anita Loomis about the O.J. Simpson case (it's included in the Neo-Futurists' *Neo Solo* book).

"Stonewalled, or The Sound of The Crowd" — Delivered as a simple monologue in *Too Much Light* in 1998; written for the annual GLBT Pride edition of the show. At the time it seemed that the human rights atrocities of the Taliban weren't being paid attention to by much of anyone except Amnesty International and the gay press.

"Davy Jones in the Produce Department: A Piscean Parable" — Staged in *Too Much Light* in 1998: I deliver the text in a chair center-stage, speaking rapid fire with occasional gasps for air. Stephanie Shaw stands behind me in a long green wig and a plastic crown of bones, and speaks the italicized words in sync with me. At the top of the piece she starts a metronome ticking rapidly, which continues underneath the piece until she stops it suddenly on the final word.

"X-Punch 2K" — Staged in *Too Much Light* in 1998, as follows: I kneel behind a long folding table on its side to suggest the "brick wall." Ernie, Cookie Monster and the Boxing Alien puppet are manipulated from behind the table by Greg Allen, John Pierson and Heather Riordan respectively. I speak all the text, without special voices for the characters. Puppet movement is carefully controlled and minimal, so as not to push the piece too far into comedy. When Cookie Monster "dies," he is draped gently over the side of the "wall."

"I ≠ AM" — The opening piece to *Talking to Myself* in 1997. Accompanied by an ambient Christoff composition, with appropriately moody lighting that created a sense of shadows in motion.

"Talking to Myself" — Originally staged in *Too Much Light* in 1990, this became the title piece to the full-length *Talking to Myself* in 1997. The *Too Much Light* staging had me addressing myself in full-length mirrors held by Spencer Kayden and Phil Ridarelli; we changed position to create a different stage picture for each of the six sections of the piece. The *Talking to Myself* staging featured a surreal video by Kurt Heintz and electronic music by Alex Christoff.

"Big Glass Jar, or Pearls Go with Everything" — First staged in *Too Much Light* in 1995, and also featured in *Talking to Myself*. In both shows, the text was spoken over a rhythmic musical background — the chorus-like verbal repetition in the piece is there as part of the interplay between text and music. In *Too Much Light*, the music was created by other cast members blowing into bottles, playing percussive instruments and singing softly; they also supplied the falsetto voices of the sea creatures. In *Talking to Myself*, I performed the piece with music by Alex Christoff and an aquatic video by Kurt Heintz.

"Snow" — Performed in *Talking to Myself*, with ambient music by Christoff.

"Talking to Myself: The Interview" — The thematic conclusion to *Talking to Myself*. The text given here has been revised slightly from the performance version; the original depended on references to another piece not included here.

Night Diaries

"Axolotl" — *Axolotl*: Also called the "Mexican Walking Fish." A larval amphibian (actually a kind of salamander) with feather-like gills on its neck, native to Mexico and the western U.S.; capable of living and breeding without metamorphosing from the larval state. Name comes from an Aztec word meaning "water doll." Associated with the Aztec god Xólotl, twin of Quetzalcóatl. *Aye-ayes*: Nocturnal lemurs with large eyes and elongated fingers, native to Madagascar. *Quagga*: An extinct African mammal resembling a small zebra, but striped only on the head, neck and front part of the body.

The Desires of Glass

The poems in this section are presented in roughly chronological order, moving backward from the most recent to the earliest.

"I Am the Man Vermeer Painted Over" — Written shortly after visiting the Metropolitan Museum of Art in New York, in summer of 1995, and seeing the painting *A Girl Asleep* (also various called *A Maid Asleep*, *A Sleeping Young Woman*, and *A Drunken Sleeping Maid at a Table*). A placard on the wall next to the painting said that radiographs had revealed the figure of a man standing "framed in the doorway," and subsequently painted over. At the time I'm writing this note, in June 2002, the museum's Web site says that there's a painted-over dog in the doorway, and the painted-over man is "in the background." Not sure if he's in the doorway, too, or not. Regardless, he's there somewhere. Someday I'll have to write a sequel from the perspective of the dog. ("Where Are the Table Scraps Vermeer Painted Over?")

"Laughing Sal" — Performed in the original *Pansy Kings' Cotillion*, 1994. Written after a trip to San Francisco during which I slept beside a monstrously huge iguana in a tank. The poem borrows, as its cast of supporting players, the denizens of San Francisco's Musée Mecanique. The Musée is a surreal and striking collection of antique arcade machines, including the coin-operated wizards and execution scenes mentioned. The Musée's most famous and beguiling resident is Laughing Sal, an enormous figure of a grinning woman who rocks and shakes to the sound of recorded laughter. *Gold lamé handkerchief*: in gay "hanky code," indicates a preference for musclemen.

"The Sideshow" — ...*Blood and semen*: There is a story that, on seeing Verlaine and Rimbaud together, Madame Verlaine cried, "There they are, covered with blood and semen!" The phrase takes on a somewhat different resonance in the age of AIDS.

"Staring at Orion's Left Foot" — Staged in *The Collapsible Detachable Self-Cleaning Universe Show*, 1993. Performed in a front of a large projection of the constellation, with suitably reflective music by Christoff.

"Map of the Body" — First performed in *Blushing Under the Mushroom*, 1992.

"Letter (Midnight presses an enormous face)" — The phrase "dear love of comrades" is from "I Hear It Was Charged Against Me" by Walt Whitman.

"A Trick of the Light" — Staged in *Too Much Light* in 1991. Spencer Kayden, Phil Ridarelli and I sat in a row of three chairs to suggest a sofa, and each spoke a stanza at a time. We were lit by two television sets tuned to static, held by other performers who moved them slowly around us to vary the lighting.

"Lisa Goddamn" — Staged in *Too Much Light*, in 1990, under the title "Direct Dial;" performed by Lisa Buscani and Ted Bales. The title is a reference to Lisa's much-performed poem about Bette Davis, "Mother Goddamn."

"The Buddha Receiving a Gift of Heart-Shaped Chocolates" — Performed in *Blushing Under the Mushroom*, 1992; also many times in *Too Much Light*.

"Van Gogh" — Written in 1989 after seeing Paul Cox's intoxicating film *Vincent*, based on the letters and diaries of Van Gogh.

"two poems appassionata" — The second poem was staged under the title "The Sea Recedes Like Sleep," in *The Collapsible Detachable Self-Cleaning Universe Show*, 1992. Reprised in *The Pansy Kings' Cotillion*, 1994. The text was reworked somewhat to add repetition of certain phrases. Performed to music by Alex Christoff and King Spill, with the wordless singing of Kathleen Puls, and a black-and-white Armando Vasquez film of the tide coming in (and then, by the magic of a film projector run backwards, going out again).

"lughnassadh iii" — *Lughnassadh*: Celtic name for the August 1 pagan holiday, also called Lammas; ritual death of the sun god. Performed in *Parts of Me Function Like a Dream*, music by Alex Christoff and vocals by Kathleen Puls.

"Letter to Carl Jung in Vienna" — In *Symbols of Transformation*, Jung analyzes the fantasies of a young American woman referred to by the pseudonym Miss Frank Miller. In the chapter "The Song of the Moth," Jung discusses a poem written by Miller entitled "The Moth to the Sun," in which the moth longs for the sun: "...But to approach thy glory; then, having gained/One raptured glance, I'll die content..."